# the fertility journal

## A Day-By-Day Guide to Getting Pregnant

Kim Hahn and the Editors of *Conceive Magazine*
Foreword by Dr. Geoffrey Sher, Obstetrician and Gynecologist

CHRONICLE BOOKS
SAN FRANCISCO

Text and illustrations © 2008 by Intellectual Capital Productions, Inc.

All rights reserved. No part of this book may be reproduced in any form without written permission from the publisher.

Library of Congress Cataloging-in-Publication Data available.

ISBN: 978-0-8118-6245-5

Manufactured in China

Design by Patrick Greenish
Indexed by Michelle Graye

Based on articles written from Fall 2004 to Fall 2007 for *Conceive Magazine*: Founder, Kim Hahn; Editor-in-Chief, Beth Weinhouse; Managing Editor, Stephanie Pancratz; Art Director, Patrick Greenish.

10 9 8 7 6 5 4 3 2 1

Chronicle Books LLC
680 Second Street
San Francisco, California 94107
www.chroniclebooks.com

www.conceiveonline.com

conceive
magazine.

# contents

Foreword . . . . . . . . . . . . . . . . . . . . . . . . . . . . . . . . . . . . . . . . . . 4
How to Use *The Fertility Journal* . . . . . . . . . . . . . . . . . . . . . . . 6
Fertility Basics . . . . . . . . . . . . . . . . . . . . . . . . . . . . . . . . . . . . 8
   Month 1: The Preconception Checkup . . . . . . . . . . . . . . . 22
   Month 2: Eat to Conceive! . . . . . . . . . . . . . . . . . . . . . . . . 32
   Month 3: Vitamins and Nutritional Supplements . . . . . . . . . . . . 42
   Month 4: Kick the Habit . . . . . . . . . . . . . . . . . . . . . . . . . . 52
   Month 5: Weighting for Pregnancy . . . . . . . . . . . . . . . . . . 62
   Month 6: Sex! . . . . . . . . . . . . . . . . . . . . . . . . . . . . . . . . . 72
   Month 7: Fertility for Him . . . . . . . . . . . . . . . . . . . . . . . . 82
   Month 8: De-stress for Success! . . . . . . . . . . . . . . . . . . . . 92
   Month 9: Get Up and Move It . . . . . . . . . . . . . . . . . . . . . 102
   Month 10: Pamper Yourself . . . . . . . . . . . . . . . . . . . . . . . 112
   Month 11: Relationship Rx . . . . . . . . . . . . . . . . . . . . . . . 122
   Month 12: Preparing for Parenthood . . . . . . . . . . . . . . . . 132
When You Need a Little Help (Fertility Treatments) . . . . . . . . . . . . 142
   Alphabet Soup (Fertility Vocabulary) . . . . . . . . . . . . . . . . 149
   How to Use This Section . . . . . . . . . . . . . . . . . . . . . . . . 150
   Fertility Treatment Cycle 1 . . . . . . . . . . . . . . . . . . . . . . . 152
   Getting through the Dreaded TWW (Two-Week Wait) . . . . . . . 164
   Fertility Treatment Cycle 2 . . . . . . . . . . . . . . . . . . . . . . . 168
   It's Very Frustrating (IVF) . . . . . . . . . . . . . . . . . . . . . . . . 180
   What Comes Next . . . . . . . . . . . . . . . . . . . . . . . . . . . . . 183
Baby on the Way . . . . . . . . . . . . . . . . . . . . . . . . . . . . . . . . . 184
Questions for Your Doctor . . . . . . . . . . . . . . . . . . . . . . . . . . 188
Contacts . . . . . . . . . . . . . . . . . . . . . . . . . . . . . . . . . . . . . . . 194
Resources . . . . . . . . . . . . . . . . . . . . . . . . . . . . . . . . . . . . . 198
Index . . . . . . . . . . . . . . . . . . . . . . . . . . . . . . . . . . . . . . . . . 202
About the Author . . . . . . . . . . . . . . . . . . . . . . . . . . . . . . . . 206

# foreword

Over the past four decades I've dedicated most of my career to reproductive health care. During this wonderful, personal, and professional journey, I've participated in reproductive medicine as a caregiver, a scientific investigator, and a patient advocate. In all these capacities I've come to realize that what patients really need is comprehensive and comprehensible information, which is often not readily available.

The desire for a child is a powerful and instinctive one with cultural, social, and psychological implications. Pregnancy is one of the most important life journeys, and navigating it successfully depends as much upon proper "planning for the trip" as on "taking the ride." In fact, not planning appropriately for pregnancy and parenthood often has serious consequences for the health of the mother and her child, and for their quality of life after birth. Yet millions of couples who are planning to conceive or have already embarked on this important journey can't find accurate and easily understandable data, leaving them to depend on whatever information they can gather from a variety of sources, not all reliable.

*The Fertility Journal: A Day-by-Day Guide to Getting Pregnant* addresses a full spectrum of reproductive issues, from planning a pregnancy to the recognition of factors affecting fertility. It also offers practical guidelines on lifestyle, diet, and nutrition. The authors unravel complicated medical, social, and psychological issues and explain them in plain English so that you can focus on a healthy and joyous pregnancy and parenthood. Every page of this journal provides accurate and concise information, coupled with the straight talk you need.

I congratulate *Conceive Magazine* on this splendid contribution. If I could make one general recommendation to every couple of reproductive age whether fertile or infertile: use the information in *The Fertility Journal*. It provides an excellent road map for a very important journey.

—*Geoffrey Sher, M.D.*
*The Sher Institutes for Reproductive Medicine (SIRM)*
*www.haveababy.com*

# how to use this book

This journal is for you. It's a place for you to record anything and everything related to getting pregnant—your menstrual cycle, your basal body temperature, your ovulation date, your vitamins, your medications, and your thoughts and feelings about "trying" and about impending parenthood.

There's no right or wrong way to use this book; you decide what works best. You can start at the beginning, read through to the first month of calendar pages, and start recording your journey. Or you can flip through and dip into the fertility and conception information at any point.

The first part of the book features an introduction with general reproductive and fertility information, and then twelve months of calendar pages. Each month has a theme, such as diet, vitamins, or exercise, with valuable information for improving your chances of success. It takes couples an average of eight months to get pregnant naturally, and after a year of trying—meaning unprotected sexual intercourse—it's time to seek medical help (earlier if you're over thirty-five). That's the reason for the year's worth of pages for you to chart your monthly cycle.

The second section of the book is for couples who are working with fertility specialists to achieve pregnancy. This section also begins with general information—about common reasons for fertility difficulties, and about the treatments that can help. The calendar pages in this section provide more space for keeping track of fertility medications and doctors' orders. And since many fertility treatments, including IUI (intrauterine insemination) and IVF (in vitro fertilization), involve a two-week wait—between insemination or embryo transfer and being able to take a pregnancy test to find out if the treatment worked—each of these treatment cycle calendar pages are followed by pages where you can record your thoughts and concerns during the waiting period.

Finally, the journal concludes with resources for further information, and information on early pregnancy, since we hope all the readers of this journal will soon get that positive pregnancy test!

But there's nothing to stop you from checking out the pregnancy pages right now, before you've even started trying. Or looking at the information in the natural conception pages even if you're already immersed in fertility treatments. The journey is yours. You determine the route.

# Fertility Basics

## Congratulations!
You've decided to become a mom, and with this journal we're here to wish you "bon voyage" on your journey to parenthood and help you along the way. You may not realize it, but you've already taken an important step toward putting the odds in your favor for an easy conception and healthy pregnancy. How did you do that? Buying this journal is an indication that you're preparing yourself—physically and psychologically—for pregnancy. "Women who plan to be pregnant and actively try to conceive have better outcomes than women who have 'Oops!' pregnancies," according to Peter Bernstein, M.D., M.P.H., a maternal-fetal specialist at Albert Einstein College of Medicine at Montefiore Medical Center in New York City.

# fertility basics

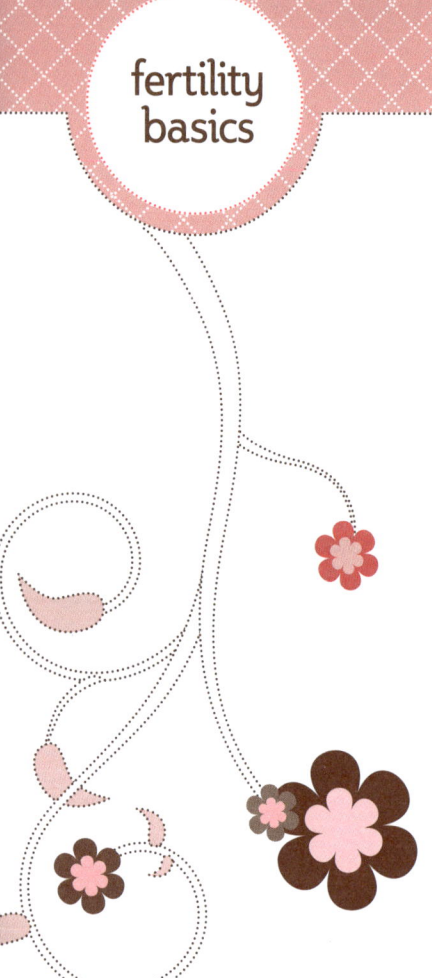

Notice that the journal contains twelve months of diary pages for charting your progress toward pregnancy. Many women assume that when they're ready to be pregnant, it will happen instantly. For some it does. But there's no need to worry if you're not one of those lucky few. In fact, it takes an average of eight months of trying for most women to get pregnant, and that's completely normal. It's also normal for conception to happen more quickly, or even much more slowly. Every couple will follow a somewhat different path to parenthood. We'd like to help you enjoy the journey.

Just as you'd tune up a car before a long trip, there are health and lifestyle factors that can help you tune up your body for conception. Taking care of your own health now will benefit your baby. It's a bit simplistic but basically true that a healthy body leads to a healthy conception and a healthy pregnancy. It's also true that there are steps you can take to boost your fertility and perhaps speed up your journey.

## pregnancy prep 101

The first step is to make a preconception visit to your doctor to let her know that you plan to start "trying" soon. If you haven't done so previously, now is the time to get chronic conditions like diabetes or thyroid problems under control, and to intercept possible problems such as polycystic ovary syndrome, endometriosis, or scarring from past sexually transmitted infections. Your doctor should also review your health history (including vaccinations), as well as your family history, to see if there are any red flags that might get in the way of a healthy pregnancy. Tell your doctor about any medications you take, to make sure they'll be safe while you're trying and during pregnancy. And by the way, encourage your guy to get himself checked out, too—after all, he's half of the conception equation! (See Month 7, beginning on page 82, for more on male fertility.)

Next take a good look at your lifestyle. Six cups of coffee a day may help you meet work project

**8 months**
The average time it takes for most women to conceive.

deadlines, but this is one project caffeine can't really help with. Drinking Cosmopolitans on girls' night out might be a lot of fun, but the time to get drinking under control is now, before you're pregnant. Most OB/GYNs say that moderate coffee consumption and an occasional alcoholic drink are fine before you're pregnant, but once you've conceived you should stop drinking alcohol entirely. (Ask your OB/GYN how he feels about caffeine during pregnancy; opinions differ.) As for smoking: QUIT NOW! Can we be any more forceful? Not only will smoking make getting pregnant much more difficult, but it will also threaten the health of your unborn child when you do conceive.

Next, make sure you're taking in all the nutrients your body needs now, and all the nutrients it will soon need for conception, and eventually for pregnancy. A healthy diet is essential, but it's also smart to start taking daily vitamins—prenatal or one-a-day type—containing folic acid. Folic acid is essential for the development of the fetus's neural tube—the earliest version of the spinal cord. Since this part of the baby's development takes place very, very early in pregnancy, it's especially important that women who are trying to conceive make sure they're taking in plenty of folic acid. If you wait until after you find out you're pregnant to begin taking the vitamins, you'll miss the benefits for an important period of your baby's development. "If women take 400 micrograms of folic acid daily prior to pregnancy, the number of spina bifida cases (a fairly common and devastating neural tube defect) can be reduced dramatically," says Margaret Comerford Freda, Ed.D., R.N., professor of obstetrics and gynecology and women's health at Albert Einstein College of Medicine at Montefiore Medical Center in New York City. Some experts recommend even more: up to 1 milligram (1,000 micrograms) of folic acid a day. Ask your doctor for his recommendation. How important is folic acid? The U.S. government's Centers for Disease Control and Prevention (CDC) considers taking folic acid to be one

# know your body

## female anatomy

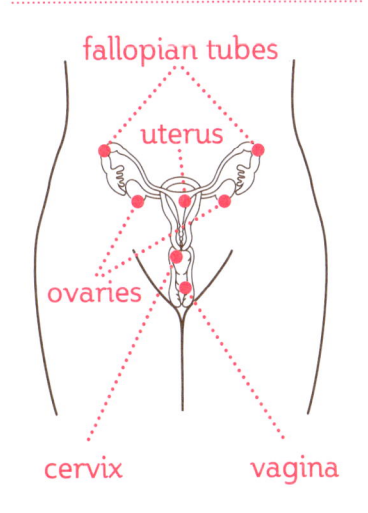

- fallopian tubes
- uterus
- ovaries
- cervix
- vagina

## male anatomy

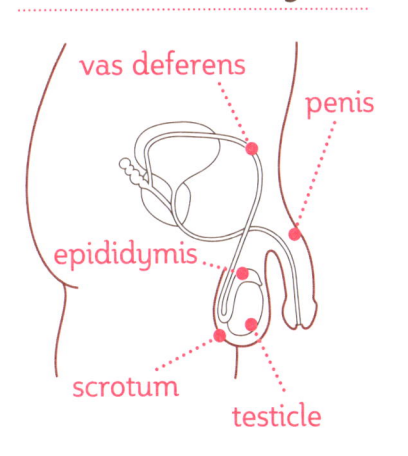

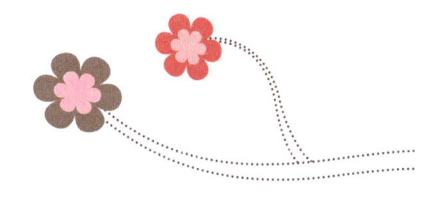

- vas deferens
- penis
- epididymis
- scrotum
- testicle

## fertility basics

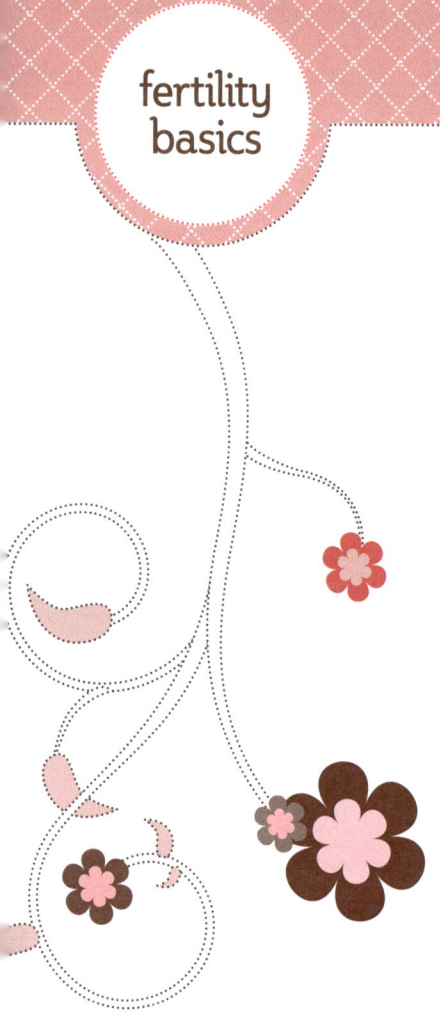

of the most important steps women can take before pregnancy, and promote it in their public health campaigns for preconception health.

Making these lifestyle changes before you start trying will give you a huge head start on a healthy pregnancy. Making them as you're trying is still a very smart step to take. In fact, even doing some of these things after you're pregnant—like quitting smoking—is better than not doing them at all.

### turbo charge your fertility

Ancient people worshipped fertility goddesses and celebrated spring fertility rituals to encourage conception, but now we know there are more scientifically sound things we can do to boost natural fertility. Most of them are surprisingly easy:

### 1. eat to conceive

Choose foods rich in whole grains, rather than refined grains (such as white bread, white rice, regular pasta, etc.). Whole grains contain bran and germ, which contain many key nutrients. Try to eat a variety of grains, too. Julia Indichova, a fertility educator and activist, calls millet "the fertility wonder grain, highly touted as a hormone balancer."

While going on a strict no-carb diet wouldn't be wise now, foods with a low glycemic index—meaning they convert to sugar more slowly in the body—is a good idea. These foods help regulate the hormone insulin in the body, and that can have a big impact on fertility.

Fruits and vegetables—preferably ones with a low glycemic index—are also important, since they're full of antioxidants and phytochemicals, which are important for overall health and fertility.

Even the types of fat you consume can make a difference. Essential fatty acids are components of all cell membranes, including those of the egg and sperm. According to Bridget Swinney, M.S., R.D., a dietitian in El Paso, Texas, most Americans consume too many omega-6 fatty acids (found in corn oil, safflower oil,

**400 micrograms**
The amount of folic acid to take everyday to dramatically reduce your baby's risk of spina bifida, a fairly common and devastating neural tube defect.

sunflower oil) and not enough omega-3s (in fish oil, canola oil, olive oil, and flaxseed). Eating salmon once or twice a week, or eggs fortified with omega-3s, is a good way to get this important nutrient.

More on fats: You've probably heard that trans fats are bad for your heart (they raise "bad" cholesterol, lower the "good," and increase the risk of heart disease. But a 2007 study at the Harvard School of Public Health in Boston has found that these fats may have another negative effect. The study found that the more trans fats a woman consumes, the greater her risk of fertility problems. Read package labels carefully and avoid foods that contain margarine or hydrogenated or partially hydrogenated vegetable oils as an ingredient. Even foods that tout zero grams of trans fat are allowed by law to contain up to half a gram, and since even small amounts of these fats can cause problems, it's best to eliminate them from your diet completely.

> The more trans fats a woman consumes, the greater her risk of fertility problems. Read package labels carefully and avoid foods that contain margarine or hydrogenated or partially hydrogenated vegetable oils as an ingredient.

## 2. weight for pregnancy

Mothers come in all shapes and sizes, but women's bodies are at their most fertile when they're at a healthy weight—not too heavy, not too thin. According to Helen Kim, M.D., an assistant professor of obstetrics and gynecology and director of the in vitro fertilization program at the University of Chicago, women who have a low body mass index (BMI) take four times as long to get pregnant as women in the normal range (18.5 to 24.9). On the other hand, women who are overweight (a BMI between 25 and 29.9; obese is 30 and over) may develop insulin resistance, meaning that too much insulin circulates in the

# fertility basics

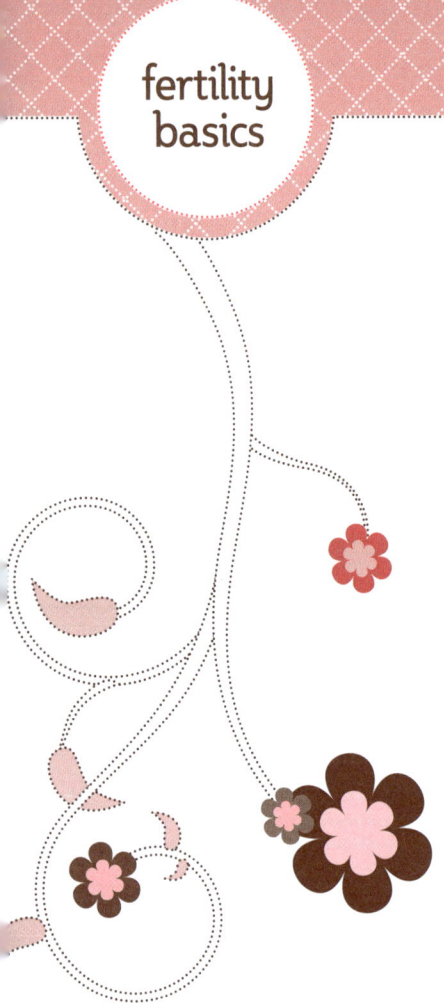

body, disrupting menstruation. Estrogen production from fat cells can also affect the ovaries and prevent eggs from being released. To calculate your BMI, take your weight in pounds, and divide it by your height in inches, squared. Take that number and multiply it by 703. Or check the Resources section on page 198 for an address of an online BMI calculator.

You don't have to starve yourself or stuff yourself in order to make a fertility difference. If you're overweight, losing just 5 to 10 percent of your current body weight is often enough to do the trick. If you're underweight, gaining as little as five pounds can sometimes jumpstart ovulation. Whatever you do, use common sense. Now is not the time to start a fad diet, or to gorge yourself on empty calories. Slow, steady, and sensible is the way to go.

## 3. supplement your efforts

In addition to a daily prenatal or one-a-day-type vitamin containing folic acid, there are fertility supplements on the market that claim to help women conceive. These supplements need to be studied more carefully, but there is some evidence that they can help. In 2004 a team of researchers at Stanford University in California found that women who took a supplement containing chasteberry (also called vitex) were more likely to get pregnant than women who didn't. The researchers found that the herb helped improve ovulation and restore hormone balance. But check with your doctor before taking any of these fertility preparations. Some women, such as those who are taking fertility drugs, should not use these supplements.

## 4. reduce your stress

No, it's not as simple as "just relax and you'll get pregnant" (and we know how incredibly annoying that phrase is when you're trying to conceive). But there is some evidence that stress can wreak havoc with hormones. And having your hormones in balance, of course, is necessary for conception. Keep

**5 to 10 percent**
The amount of your current body weight that you may need to lose to make a fertility difference.

reminding yourself that it takes women an average of eight months to conceive, and that five out of six couples won't have a problem getting pregnant. And if work stress or personal problems have you tense, stress-reduction techniques like yoga, imagery, meditation, massage, or just knitting in front of the television or taking a walk with your partner can help keep you centered and stress-free.

## cycle savvy

You probably haven't thought a lot about the biology of menstruation since that awkward presentation around the fifth grade, when a nurse came to your school to tell you that "Soon, you will be a woman!" After that it was on to high school health class, where the emphasis was most definitely on how NOT to get pregnant. For a while most women see their periods—and cramps—as an excuse to get out of gym class. Then it becomes welcome confirmation each month that you're not pregnant. But now you're at a point in your life when you realize you want to be pregnant, and nothing you've been taught has prepared you for how to use your cycle to conceive. We're going to do that right now.

Here's the short version: Timing is everything. Perfect eggs and flawless sperm are useless if they don't hook up at the opportune moment. To make that happen, you have to have sexual intercourse on the day of ovulation (the point in the cycle when the ripened egg is released from the ovary and then travels down the fallopian tubes to the uterus), or up to a few days before (since sperm can survive in the female reproductive tract for several days). Miss the dates and you've missed your chance, at least for that cycle.

That's why fertility experts recommend that couples

**In fact, ovulation occurs not 14 days after menstruation begins, but 14 days before.**

# fertility basics

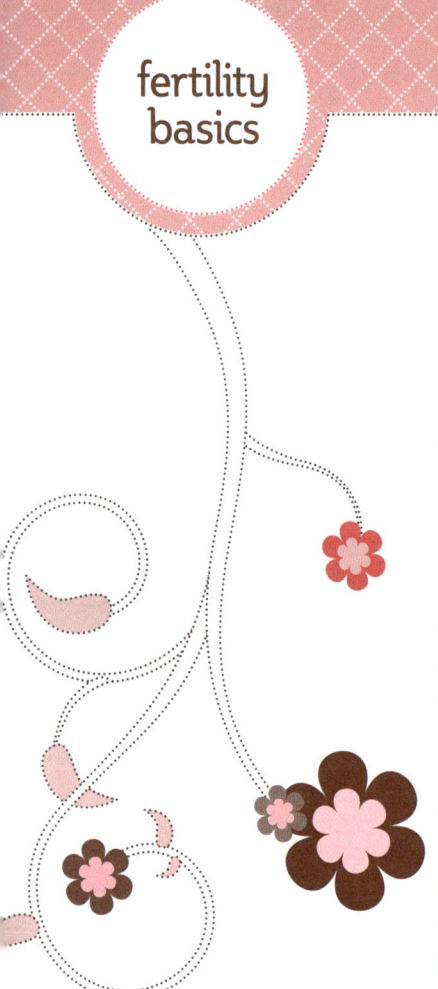

trying to conceive have sexual intercourse every other day starting about a week before ovulation each cycle. That way, you're sure to have sex at least once during your fertile period each menstrual cycle. Also, by ejaculating every other day, your partner will keep his sperm supply "fresh" without depleting it too quickly. Too-frequent ejaculation can lower sperm count slightly.

But if making love every other day—probably for a few months—doesn't sound feasible or even appealing, you might want to try to figure out exactly when you're ovulating so you can concentrate your baby-making efforts around that time. Here are four ways to pinpoint your most fertile time; choose the one you think will work best for you.

## 1. chart your menstrual cycle

One of the most common misconceptions about fertility is that every woman ovulates on day 14 of her menstrual cycle. Actually, that's true only for women with a regular 28-day cycle. So if you're pinning your hopes on conceiving by having sex with your partner each cycle around day 14, you may be in for a long wait. In fact, ovulation occurs not 14 days *after* menstruation begins, but 14 days *before*. So if you have a very regular cycle, you can estimate your date of ovulation by subtracting two weeks from the date of your next expected period. For example: A woman with a regular 30-day cycle probably ovulates around day 16; a woman with a regular 26-day cycle, around day 12.

## 2. take your temperature

Charting your basal body temperature (BBT)—your morning body temperature before you get out of bed—is another way to pinpoint ovulation. A woman's normal, nonovulating temperature is between 96 and 99 degrees Fahrenheit, depending on the individual. But following the release of an egg, BBT increases by about half a degree, and remains slightly elevated until right before menstruation. "Charting

**18.5 to 24.9**
The normal range of body mass index (BMI), where women's bodies are at their most fertile.

your temperature helps you better gauge your window of opportunity to maximize fertility," says Lawrence Werlin, M.D., director of Coastal Fertility Medical Center in Irvine, California. And if you chart it for a few cycles, it may help you to predict ovulation if your cycle is regular.

If you're interested in charting your BBT, you'll need a special thermometer that measures BBT in tenths of a degree; these are inexpensive and widely available in drugstores. To get an accurate BBT reading, follow these steps:

1. Take your temperature when you first wake up and are lying or sitting quietly in bed. You need to do the reading at the same time, give or take 30 minutes, every morning.
2. Leave the thermometer on your night table before you go to bed so there's no need to get up for it in the morning. Shake mercury thermometers down at night or dip them briefly in cool water. Doing the motions in the morning can cause a rise in temperature.
3. Don't eat or drink anything, even water, before doing the reading.
4. Be aware of factors other than ovulation that can increase BBT: emotional disturbance, stress, a cold or infection, jet lag, drinking alcohol the night before, using an electric blanket.
5. Don't pull all-nighters: You need to have at least three hours of uninterrupted sleep to get an accurate reading.

Unfortunately, BBT isn't the best way to time sexual intercourse for conception. By the time your BBT rises, there's little fertile time left to conceive. So BBT charting is more helpful to reassure you that you are actually ovulating each month, and if your cycle is regular it may allow you to predict the next cycle's most fertile time.

> Timing is everything. Perfect eggs and flawless sperm are useless if they don't hook up at the opportune moment. Miss the dates and you've missed your chance, at least for that cycle.

# fertility basics

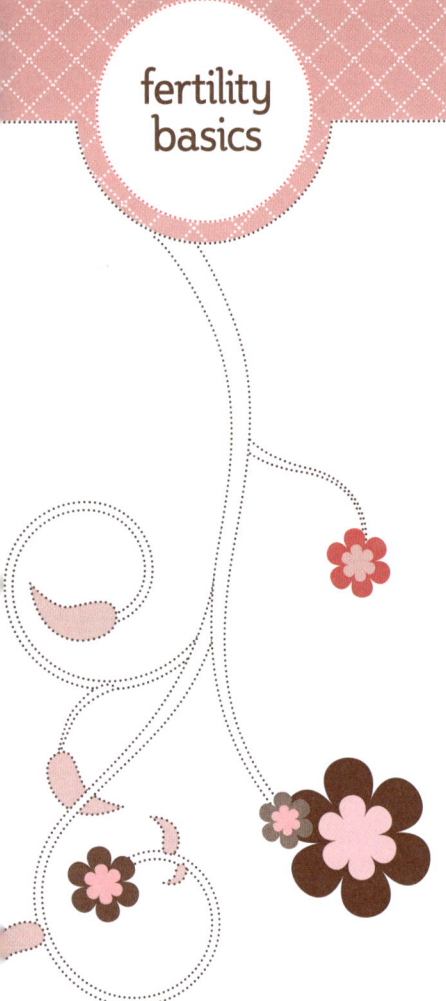

### 3. check your cervical mucus

Okay, we admit it sounds pretty gross. But if you can force yourself to get over the "yuck" factor you'll have access to a free and easy method of ovulation detection. Cervical mucus (we'll just call it CM, because it sounds better), can give you insight into your cycle without the need for any special instruments or measuring devices other than your own sense of sight and touch. You can examine these secretions by feel or appearance—in your underwear or on a piece of toilet paper—to find out where you are in your cycle. For a few days after your period, your CM may be dry or sticky, then it starts to get wetter. When it becomes slippery and stretchy (it's often compared to a raw egg white), that's when you're most fertile.

### 4. use a fertility monitor

If your cycle tends to be irregular, over-the-counter ovulation predictor kits can help pinpoint your fertile phase. Most women use their morning urine to measure luteinizing hormone (LH), which surges right before ovulation. "It's a great way to maximize your chances of conception," says John R. Sussman, M.D., assistant clinical professor of obstetrics and gynecology at the University of Connecticut School of Medicine. These reasonably priced kits are available in most drugstores.

Another type of ovulation kit measures the amount of estrogen detectable in the saliva to identify ovulation. To use these monitors, a woman applies a small amount of saliva to a lens, then looks at it under a small microscope (included in the kit). A fernlike pattern indicates the fertile phase. These monitors range from simple microscopes to high-priced, automated, electronic devices.

Take your pick—any or all of these methods will help you identify the most fertile phase in your cycle. Now that you've figured out when, you know what to do, right? Not so fast. There's one last thing to take care of: Ditch the birth control.

**4 to 6 weeks** The time it takes for most women to get their first post-Pill period.

## conception and contraception

If you've been using natural family planning methods or barrier methods like the condom, diaphragm, or cervical cap, then you're good to go. These methods are all easily reversible, meaning that whenever you're not using them, your fertility is unaffected. But if you've been using hormonal methods such as the contraceptive Pill, IUD, Norplant, or vaginal ring, there are a few things you should be aware of.

Doctors consider the Pill an easily reversible method of contraception, too. Not only doesn't the Pill impair your fertility, it may actually preserve it. Your odds of developing pelvic inflammatory disease are reduced when you're on the Pill. And, what's more, the Pill can give women with endometriosis or polycystic ovary syndrome a reproductive boost when they're ready to conceive. "The Pill controls the symptoms of endometriosis (minimizing the amount of scar tissue that is formed in the fallopian tubes) and, in women with polycystic ovary syndrome, it thins out the thickened outer covering that builds up on the ovarian cortex," notes David B. Morehead, M.D., D.O., chief of obstetrics at Baylor Medical Center at Waxahachie in Waxahachie, Texas.

More good news: Most women get their first post-Pill period within four to six weeks of going off the pill, and 80 percent will be ovulating within three months (95 percent within the year).

So should you start with the baby-making program the moment you toss your Pills in the trash? Doctors used to advise women to wait for at least one normal post-Pill period before becoming pregnant in order to avoid their risk of miscarriage. Now that advice is considered unnecessary. Waiting for your first post-Pill period to arrive will make it easier to pinpoint

> **Waiting for your first post-Pill period to arrive will make it easier to pinpoint your probable date of conception, and to more accurately date your pregnancy and predict your due date.**

# fertility basics

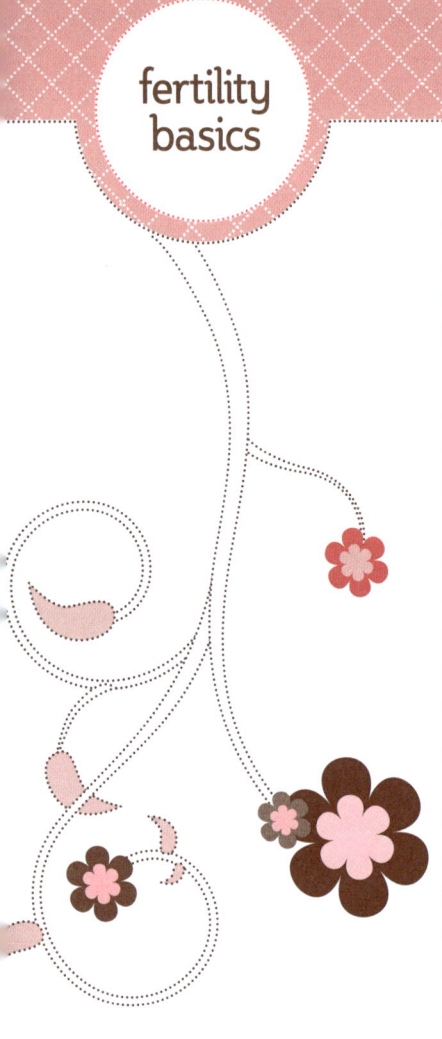

your probable date of conception, and to more accurately date your pregnancy and predict your due date. But as far as a healthy conception and pregnancy go, it's up to you how quickly you want to begin trying.

Other methods of hormonal contraception, like the Patch (which delivers hormones through the skin) or the Ring (which releases hormones through a small, flexible ring inserted into the vagina for three weeks at a time) are still fairly new and not in very wide use yet. But evidence suggests that fertility returns fairly quickly when they are removed from the body. The same is true of the IUD (intrauterine device), which may or may not contain hormones. Once it's removed, the return to fertility is fairly rapid—generally a couple of months.

But at least one other method of birth control is not intended for women who want to become pregnant any time soon. Depo-Provera is a hormonal shot injected into a woman's arms or buttocks every three months to prevent ovulation. Research has shown that the median time for the return to fertility is 10 months after the last shot (although pregnancy can occur much sooner).

## motherhood after miscarriage

The hope of conceiving with your partner, the joy of a positive pregnancy test . . . and then the devastation of a miscarriage. Considering that an estimated 15 percent of all "known" pregnancies (pregnancies confirmed with a pregnancy test) and 50 percent of all pregnancies end in miscarriage, this experience is far too common. Though it won't make the hurt go away, it's still helpful to know that early pregnancy loss occurs so frequently that many obstetricians consider it a normal part of reproduction. And the vast majority of women who suffer miscarriages go on to have normal pregnancies afterward. In fact, most doctors won't even advise a woman to have diagnostic testing until after three miscarriages, when the problem is then termed "recurrent pregnancy loss."

There are many, many reasons why miscarriages occur. Most miscarriages are isolated, random events. The cause may never be pinpointed, and it will probably not be repeated. Experts believe that approximately 60 percent of all miscarriages are caused by chromosomal abnormalities in the fetus. Pregnancy loss can also be caused by uterine abnormalities, immunologic disorders, untreated illness (such as diabetes or thyroid disorders), polycystic ovarian syndrome, bacterial infections, and some lifestyle choices (tobacco, alcohol, drugs, environmental toxins).

According to doctors, women who have a miscarriage have a better than 80 percent chance of going on to have a healthy baby. For one thing, they've already shown they can get pregnant. If you're trying to conceive again after a miscarriage and think that your pregnancy loss was caused by something preventable or treatable (such as an illness or lifestyle choice), take steps to address it. Otherwise try to approach another pregnancy with your hope and excitement intact. The odds are all in your favor.

**Early pregnancy loss occurs so frequently that many obstetricians consider it a normal part of reproduction. And the vast majority of women who suffer miscarriages go on to have normal pregnancies afterward.**

## on to month one . . .

In this journal we've included calendar pages full of places for you to chart your cycle, temperature, vitamins, and medications . We've also left space for you to do some journaling, chronicling your thoughts as you undertake this incredible journey. The pages are full of information about all aspects of preconception health and conception. Read them all; you never know which tip will be the one that does the trick.

# month 1

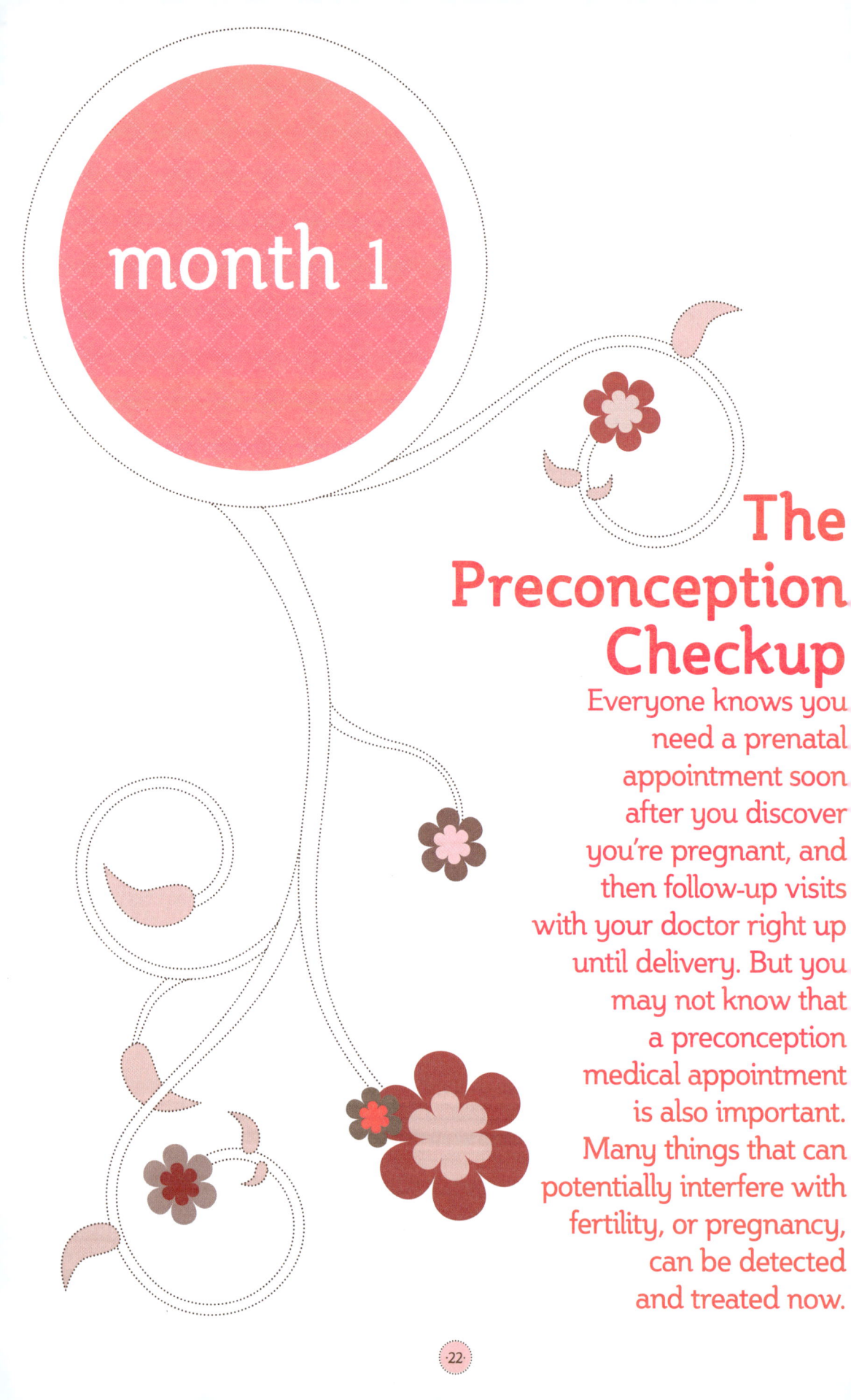

## The Preconception Checkup

Everyone knows you need a prenatal appointment soon after you discover you're pregnant, and then follow-up visits with your doctor right up until delivery. But you may not know that a preconception medical appointment is also important. Many things that can potentially interfere with fertility, or pregnancy, can be detected and treated now.

Do you go for regular OB/GYN check-ups?   ○ Yes   ○ No

How recent was your last appointment? ......................................................................
..........................................................................................................................................

Did you discuss fertility and pregnancy with your doctor?   ○ Yes   ○ No

List any existing health conditions you have: ...........................................................
..........................................................................................................................................
..........................................................................................................................................

List any medications you are taking: .........................................................................
..........................................................................................................................................
..........................................................................................................................................

Is there anything in your health history—
gynecological or otherwise—that might be a concern? ........................................
..........................................................................................................................................
..........................................................................................................................................
..........................................................................................................................................

Anything in your family health history? ...................................................................
..........................................................................................................................................
..........................................................................................................................................

Have you been pregnant before? If so, when? ........................................................
..........................................................................................................................................

# month 1 week 1

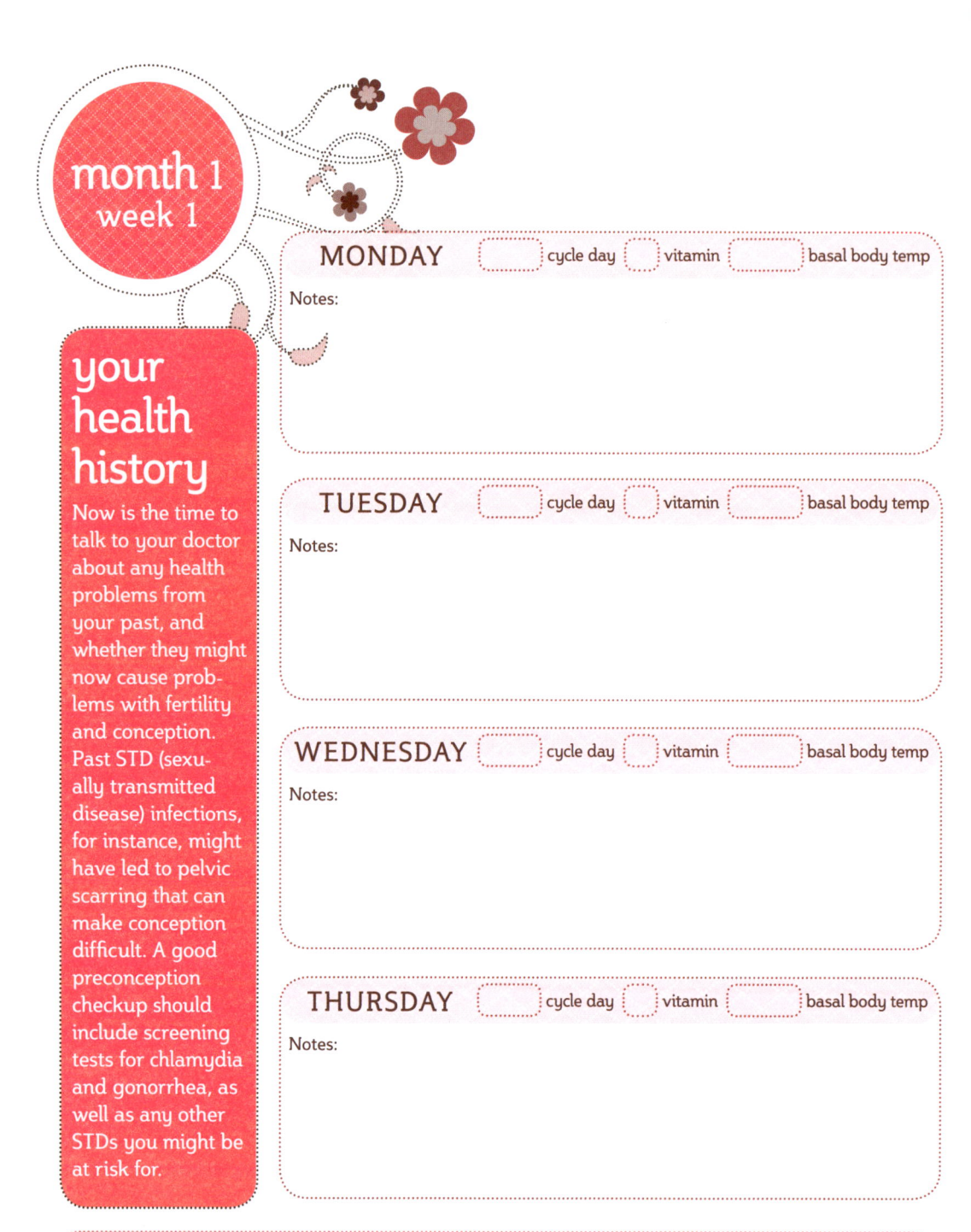

## your health history

Now is the time to talk to your doctor about any health problems from your past, and whether they might now cause problems with fertility and conception. Past STD (sexually transmitted disease) infections, for instance, might have led to pelvic scarring that can make conception difficult. A good preconception checkup should include screening tests for chlamydia and gonorrhea, as well as any other STDs you might be at risk for.

### MONDAY — cycle day — vitamin — basal body temp
Notes:

### TUESDAY — cycle day — vitamin — basal body temp
Notes:

### WEDNESDAY — cycle day — vitamin — basal body temp
Notes:

### THURSDAY — cycle day — vitamin — basal body temp
Notes:

## looking ahead to pregnancy: the first prenatal exam

When should you have your first prenatal appointment? Call your doctor as soon as you get that positive pregnancy test. If you're at high risk—because you're over thirty-five, because you had trouble conceiving, or because you have a chronic health condition—the doctor will probably want to see you right away. Otherwise you may not have that first check-up for several more weeks.

## FRIDAY  ⬚ cycle day  ⬚ vitamin  ⬚ basal body temp
Notes:

## SATURDAY  ⬚ cycle day  ⬚ vitamin  ⬚ basal body temp
Notes:

## SUNDAY  ⬚ cycle day  ⬚ vitamin  ⬚ basal body temp
Notes:

If you have had a sexually transmitted disease, you might be embarrassed to talk to your doctor about your concerns that it will affect your fertility. Don't be. Doctors have heard it all, and their job is answering your questions and treating your problems—not judging you. Ask your doctor about anything in your life—current or past—that you worry might affect your ability to get pregnant. Make a list of questions here so you won't forget.

## month 1
### week 2

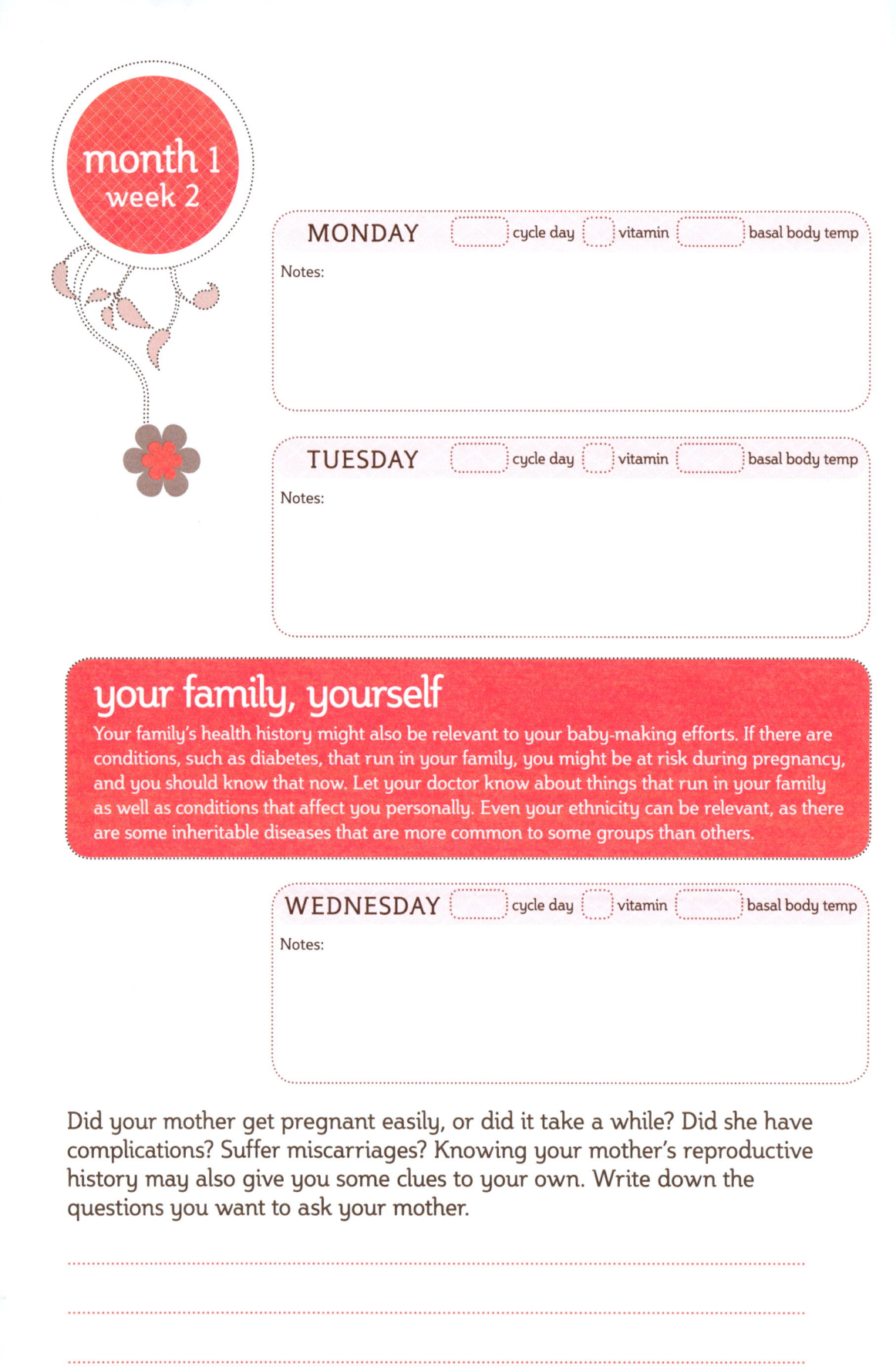

**MONDAY**  ( ) cycle day  ( ) vitamin  ( ) basal body temp
Notes:

**TUESDAY**  ( ) cycle day  ( ) vitamin  ( ) basal body temp
Notes:

### your family, yourself
Your family's health history might also be relevant to your baby-making efforts. If there are conditions, such as diabetes, that run in your family, you might be at risk during pregnancy, and you should know that now. Let your doctor know about things that run in your family as well as conditions that affect you personally. Even your ethnicity can be relevant, as there are some inheritable diseases that are more common to some groups than others.

**WEDNESDAY**  ( ) cycle day  ( ) vitamin  ( ) basal body temp
Notes:

Did your mother get pregnant easily, or did it take a while? Did she have complications? Suffer miscarriages? Knowing your mother's reproductive history may also give you some clues to your own. Write down the questions you want to ask your mother.

# looking ahead to pregnancy: doctor's orders

You may be surprised at your first prenatal visit to find out that your doctor thinks that a cup of coffee a day is no problem during pregnancy . . . although your friend's doctor made her cut out caffeine completely. Or that you should avoid haircoloring, while your friend happily kept her roots blonde for nine months. If you trust your doctor, take her advice and ignore what your friend's physician said. Every pregnancy is different, and so is every woman (and every doctor).

### THURSDAY [ ] cycle day [ ] vitamin [ ] basal body temp
Notes:

### FRIDAY [ ] cycle day [ ] vitamin [ ] basal body temp
Notes:

### SATURDAY [ ] cycle day [ ] vitamin [ ] basal body temp
Notes:

### SUNDAY [ ] cycle day [ ] vitamin [ ] basal body temp
Notes:

## month 1
### week 3

**MONDAY** ☐ cycle day ☐ vitamin ☐ basal body temp
Notes:

**TUESDAY** ☐ cycle day ☐ vitamin ☐ basal body temp
Notes:

**WEDNESDAY** ☐ cycle day ☐ vitamin ☐ basal body temp
Notes:

**THURSDAY** ☐ cycle day ☐ vitamin ☐ basal body temp
Notes:

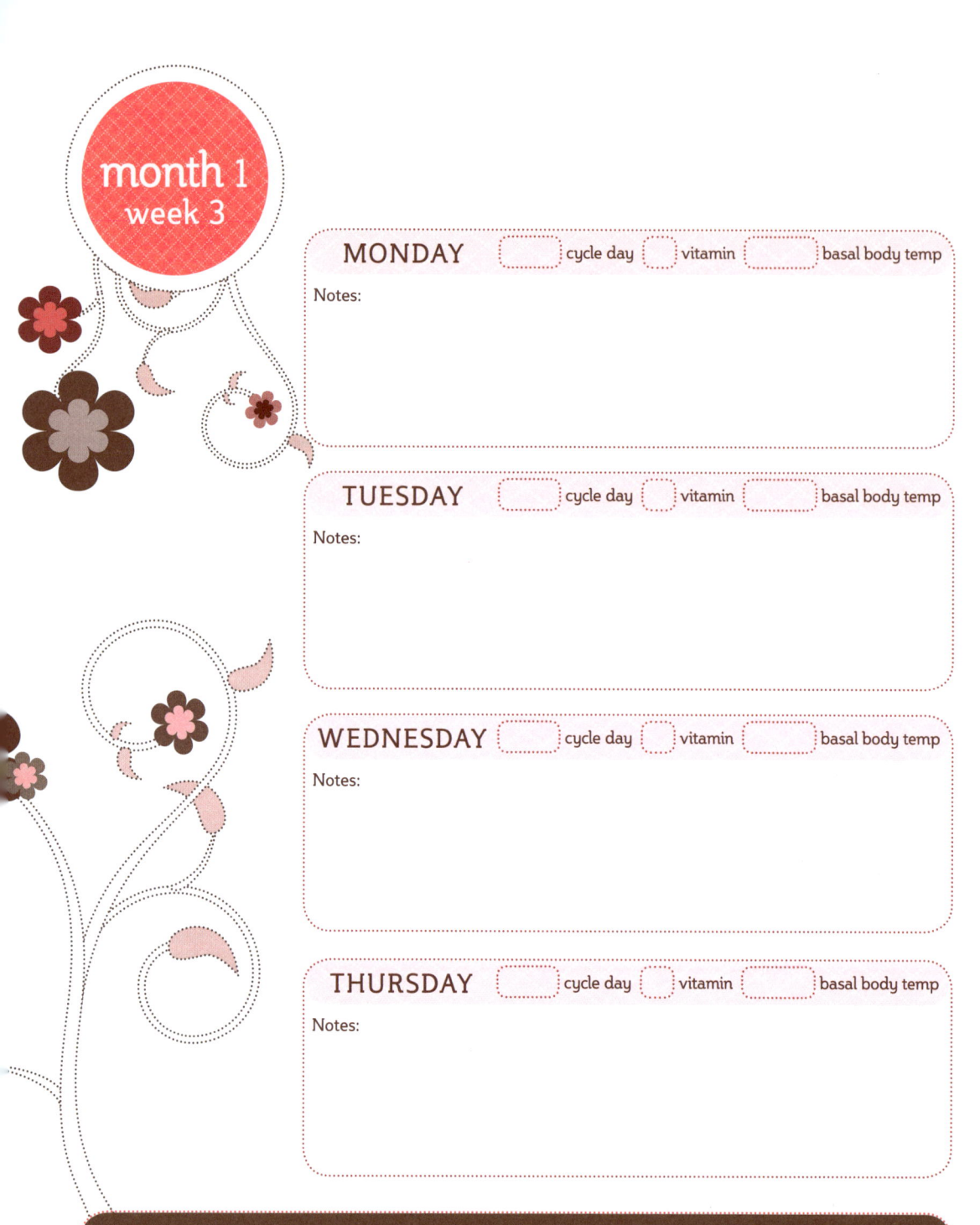

## looking ahead to pregnancy: the flu shot

Some vaccinations aren't just safe during pregnancy: they're recommended. A case in point is the flu shot. The Centers for Disease Control and Prevention (CDC) now recommends the flu shot for all pregnant women, regardless of trimester. These shots are specially formulated each year to protect against the strain of flu virus that scientists anticipate will be a risk. The shots are generally given in the fall. Ask your obstetrician for more information.

**FRIDAY**  cycle day ___  vitamin ___  basal body temp ___
Notes:

**SATURDAY**  cycle day ___  vitamin ___  basal body temp ___
Notes:

**SUNDAY**  cycle day ___  vitamin ___  basal body temp ___
Notes:

## get your shots

Be sure to bring your immunization records to your preconception appointment. Now's the time to get your vaccinations up to date. You may need a tetanus booster, for example. And you should be tested for immunity to measles, rubella (German measles), and varicella (chicken pox). If you've never had these diseases or the vaccines for them, you can have the shots before you get pregnant.

Besides a preconception medical checkup, make a dental appointment, too. Gum disease has been linked with pregnancy risks, and the time to take care of your teeth and gums is before you conceive. While you're at it, what other medical checkups can you get out of the way now? Do you need an eye exam? Did you want to fix a bunion on your foot? Were you hoping to have a dermatologic or cosmetic procedure? Write down the medical visits you want to take care of before pregnancy, and then get on the phone and set them up: There's no telling how quickly you'll conceive.

# month 1
## week 4

**MONDAY** — cycle day — vitamin — basal body temp
Notes:

**TUESDAY** — cycle day — vitamin — basal body temp
Notes:

**WEDNESDAY** — cycle day — vitamin — basal body temp
Notes:

**THURSDAY** — cycle day — vitamin — basal body temp
Notes:

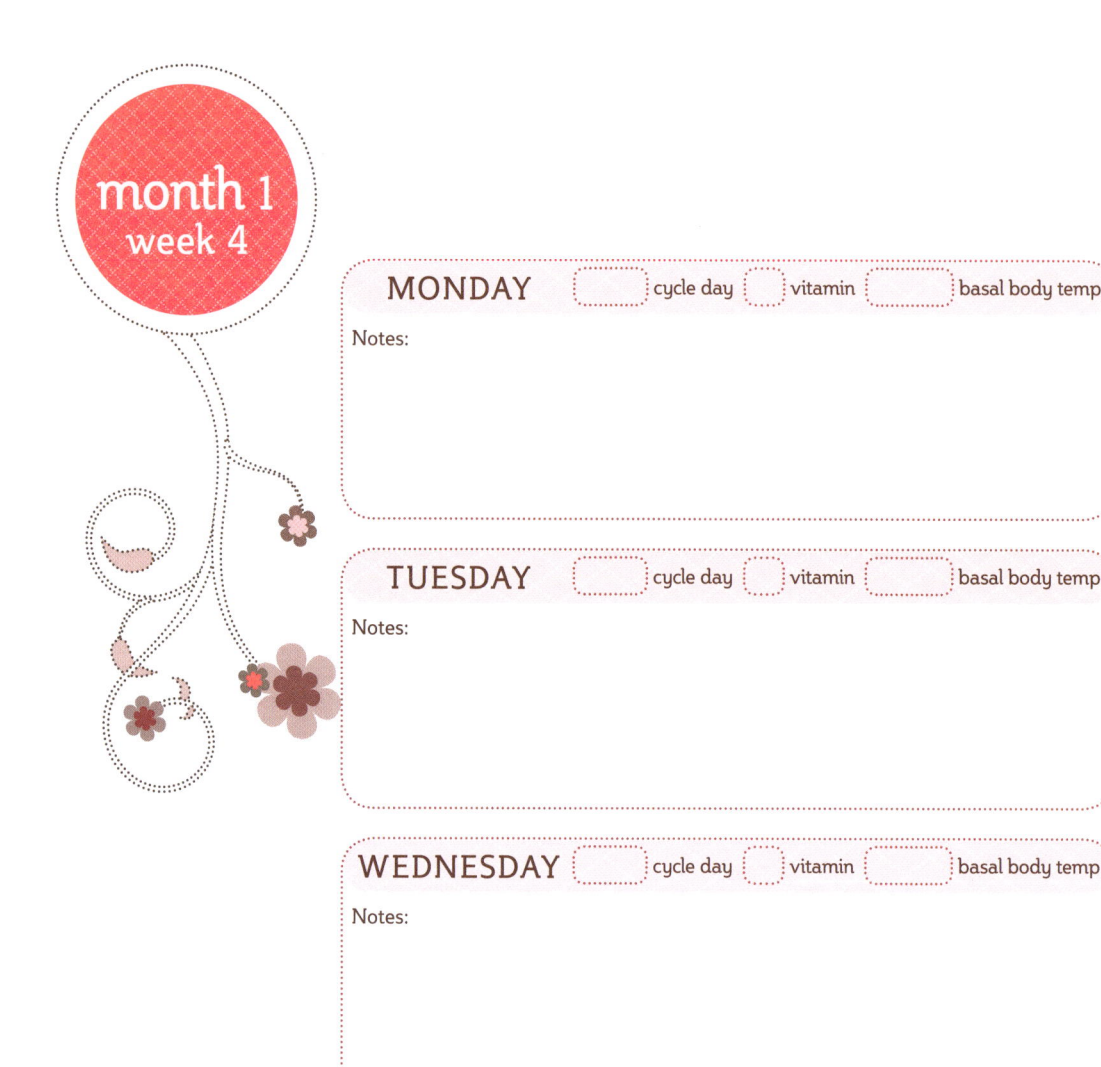

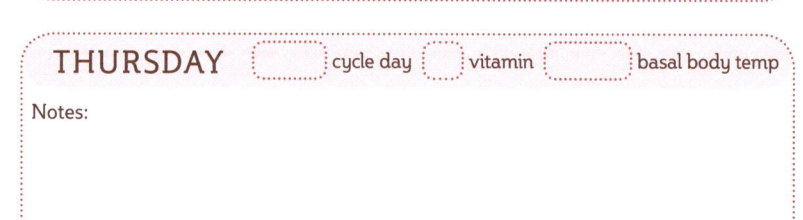

## looking ahead to pregnancy: first tests

All those preconception tests were just the beginning. Your nine months of pregnancy will be full of tests. Blood tests will help doctors establish the pregnancy is progressing normally. Ultrasound images can check the baby's heartbeat and physical development. Genetic tests can screen the baby for disorders such as Down syndrome.

**FRIDAY** ⬚ cycle day ⬚ vitamin ⬚ basal body temp

Notes:

### testing, testing

There are now tests to detect genetic carriers for dozens of hereditary conditions. The specific tests your obstetrician recommends for you will depend on your own personal and family history. If it turns out you're at risk for passing a genetic disease on to your offspring, a genetic counselor can discuss ways to help ensure your child will be healthy.

**SATURDAY** ⬚ cycle day ⬚ vitamin ⬚ basal body temp

Notes:

**SUNDAY** ⬚ cycle day ⬚ vitamin ⬚ basal body temp

Notes:

Make a list of all the medications you take, whether prescription or over-the-counter. Don't forget to include vitamins, dietary supplements, herbs, and other holistic or alternative therapies. Bring this list to your doctor when you have your checkup. You may need to stop taking some things, or find alternatives.

.............................................................................................

.............................................................................................

.............................................................................................

# month 2

## Eat to Conceive!

You're not eating for two yet, but eating to conceive is just as important. Start by kicking your bad habits and adopting some new good ones that will maximize your fertility and take you through a healthy pregnancy. Remember: The healthier you are, the healthier your baby will be, too.

What are your worst eating habits? ..............................................................................

..............................................................................................................................................

What are some strategies you could use to change these bad habits? ...............

..............................................................................................................................................

If you could just change one thing about the way you eat, what would it be?

..............................................................................................................................................

Could you make this change just one day a week? Two? Three? ........................

..............................................................................................................................................

How many servings of fruits and vegetables do you eat every day? Where could you add in extra servings if you're not getting the recommended five each day?

..............................................................................................................................................

..............................................................................................................................................

Do you eat whole grains and whole-grain breads and pastas?   ◯ Yes   ◯ No

How much water do you drink each day? ..................................................................

What's your "empty" calorie food vice? Is it soft drinks, sugary candies and cookies, greasy or salty snack foods?

..............................................................................................................................................

What emotional triggers make you crave these foods? ..........................................

..............................................................................................................................................

What could you do instead of eat to make yourself feel better? ..........................

..............................................................................................................................................

# month 2
## week 1

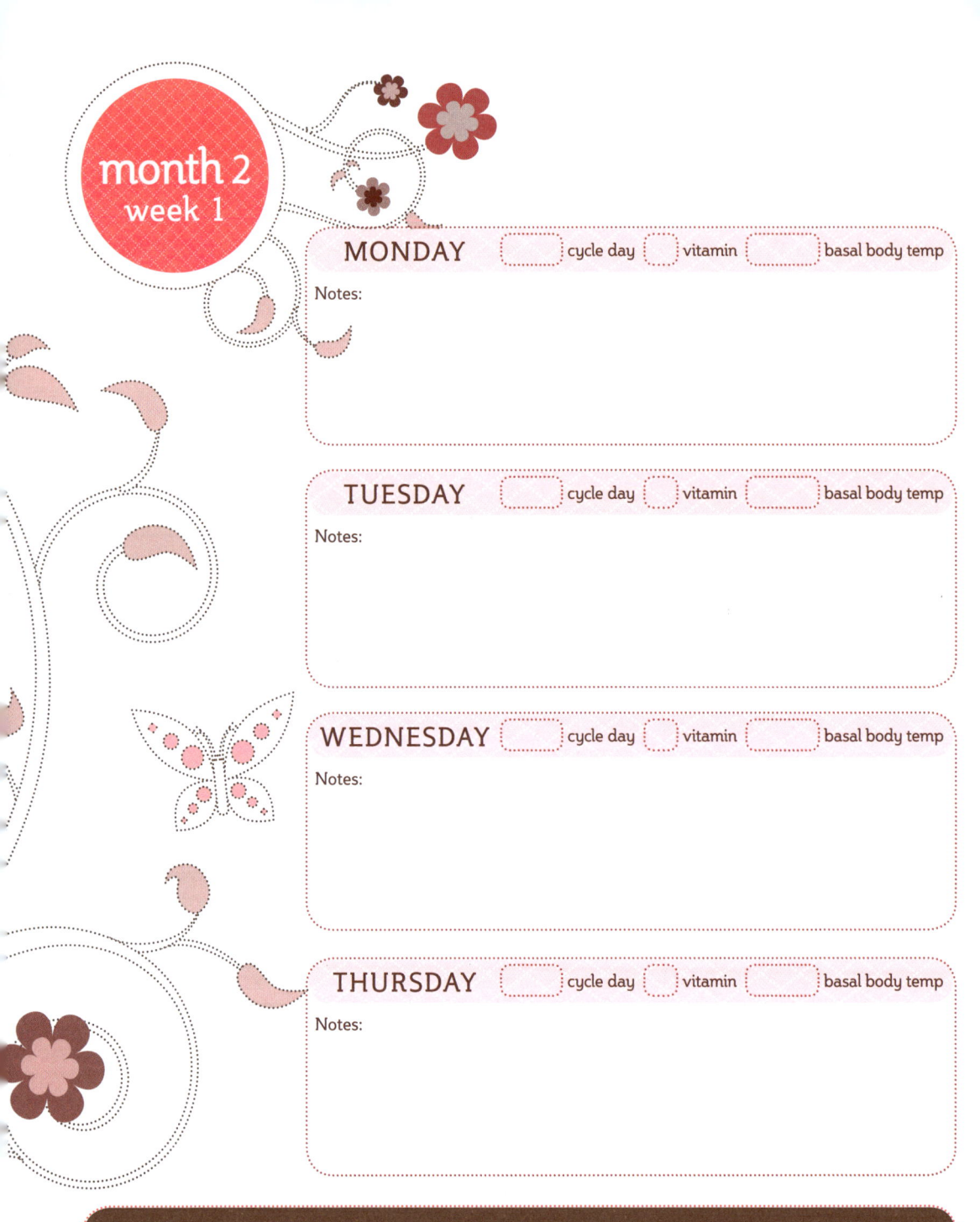

**MONDAY** | cycle day | vitamin | basal body temp
Notes:

**TUESDAY** | cycle day | vitamin | basal body temp
Notes:

**WEDNESDAY** | cycle day | vitamin | basal body temp
Notes:

**THURSDAY** | cycle day | vitamin | basal body temp
Notes:

## looking ahead to pregnancy: eating for two

Yes, there's a growing person inside of you, and he or she needs nutrition, too. But that person is extremely small. The extra metabolic needs of pregnancy are estimated as an extra 300 calories a day. Rather than meet that need with calorie-dense junk food, choose items full of the protein, iron, calcium, and other nutrients your growing baby needs. Try adding four glasses of nonfat milk, or two cups of flavored yogurt, to your pre-pregnancy diet to add vitamins and minerals along with the calories.

**FRIDAY**  ⬜ cycle day  ⬜ vitamin  ⬜ basal body temp
Notes:

**SATURDAY**  ⬜ cycle day  ⬜ vitamin  ⬜ basal body temp
Notes:

**SUNDAY**  ⬜ cycle day  ⬜ vitamin  ⬜ basal body temp
Notes:

## start keeping a food journal

You may think your diet is reasonably healthy, but once you start writing down everything you eat, you may be surprised. Keeping a daily food journal is one of the best ways to see what you're doing right, and what you should think about changing. What you're aiming for: less junk, more real food.

When you grocery shop, try to keep in mind that the healthiest foods—fresh produce, milk and dairy products, fish and chicken—tend to be around the perimeter of the store. Processed and packaged foods, which tend to have more calories, trans fats, and artificial ingredients—are more concentrated in the center aisles. List the foods you buy in the center aisles. Then list possible substitutes around the perimeter of the store.

# month 2 week 2

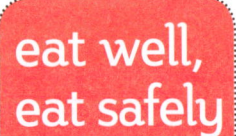

## eat well, eat safely

Pregnant women and young children are especially vulnerable to foodborne illness and contamination, and the time to safeguard your diet is before you're pregnant. Wash fruits and vegetables carefully to avoid pesticides and salmonella bacteria. Make sure meat, chicken, and eggs are well cooked. Avoid unpasteurized juices and cheeses. While fish is generally healthy, avoid fish that are high in mercury or other pollutants; see the Resources section on page 198 for more help.

### MONDAY — cycle day — vitamin — basal body temp
Notes:

### TUESDAY — cycle day — vitamin — basal body temp
Notes:

### WEDNESDAY — cycle day — vitamin — basal body temp
Notes:

### THURSDAY — cycle day — vitamin — basal body temp
Notes:

### FRIDAY — cycle day — vitamin — basal body temp
Notes:

# looking ahead to pregnancy: cravings

Not all pregnant women experience food cravings, but many do. Others experience the opposite of cravings: food aversions. Both cravings and aversions are simply different ways that changing food tastes express themselves during pregnancy. Most of these changes are harmless, but if you experience changes that concern you, check with your doctor.

**SATURDAY**  ⬚ cycle day  ⬚ vitamin  ⬚ basal body temp

Notes:

**SUNDAY**  ⬚ cycle day  ⬚ vitamin  ⬚ basal body temp

Notes:

Do you have a favorite risky food, such as runny eggs, unwashed fruit, or rare meat? ............

Which of your favorite foods (even sushi!) will you need to give up now through delivery? ............

How can you reward yourself with a healthy treat instead?

# month 2
## week 3

**MONDAY** — cycle day — vitamin — basal body temp
Notes:

**TUESDAY** — cycle day — vitamin — basal body temp
Notes:

**WEDNESDAY** — cycle day — vitamin — basal body temp
Notes:

**THURSDAY** — cycle day — vitamin — basal body temp
Notes:

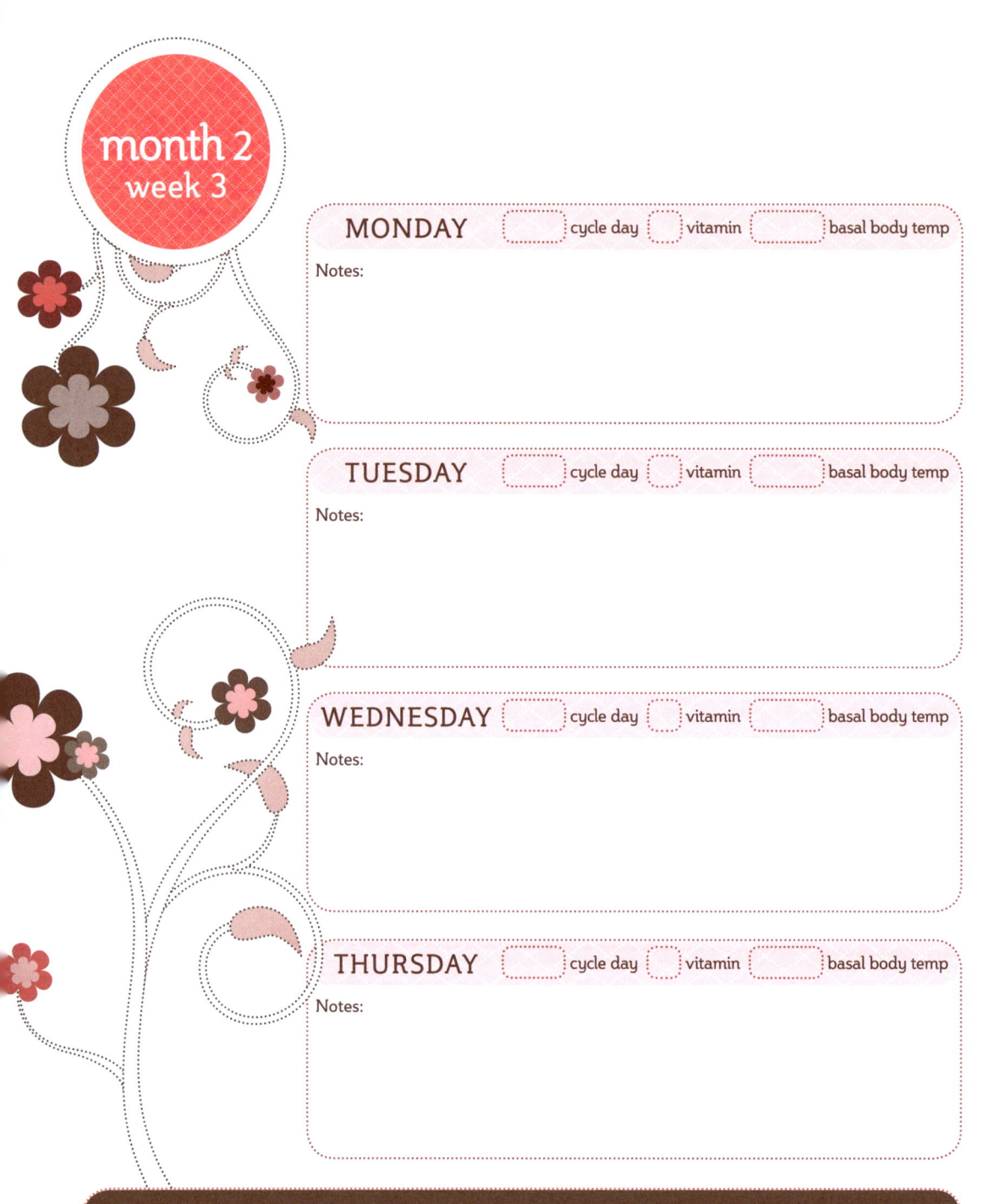

## looking ahead to pregnancy: a wake-up call for healthy eating

If you took a good look at your diet and made healthy changes while you were trying to conceive, you're ahead of the game. Keep doing what you're doing and follow your obstetrician's advice. But if you were postponing some of the tougher changes—giving up rare burgers, sushi, swordfish steaks, sugary snacks with empty calories, etc.—there's no more time to wait. Now you're feeding your baby, too, and nothing's more important than getting your child off to the best possible start.

### FRIDAY  ◯ cycle day  ◯ vitamin  ◯ basal body temp
Notes:

### SATURDAY  ◯ cycle day  ◯ vitamin  ◯ basal body temp
Notes:

### SUNDAY  ◯ cycle day  ◯ vitamin  ◯ basal body temp
Notes:

What are you thinking and feeling when you make unhealthy and healthy food choices?

..............................................................................
..............................................................................
..............................................................................

How can you change the thoughts and feelings that lead to "bad" eating?

..............................................................................
..............................................................................
..............................................................................

## fats and fertility

As if trans fats didn't have a bad enough rap—they're known to raise "bad" cholesterol, lower "good" cholesterol, and increase risk of heart disease—a Harvard study has found that the more trans fats a woman eats, the greater her risk of fertility problems. Eliminate them from your diet by avoiding most margarines, vegetable shortening, partially hydrogenated vegetable oils, fried chips, many fast foods, and most commercial baked goods. Check food package labels for more information.

# month 2
## week 4

**MONDAY** — cycle day — vitamin — basal body temp

Notes:

**TUESDAY** — cycle day — vitamin — basal body temp

Notes:

## be carb smart

Low- or no-carb fad diets aren't a good idea for women who are trying to get pregnant, but learning to balance carbohydrates, protein, and fat to help the body naturally regulate the hormone insulin may help with conception. Start by choosing carbs that are lower on the glycemic index (meaning they convert to sugar more slowly). See the Resources section beginning on page 198 to find online lists of these foods.

**WEDNESDAY** — cycle day — vitamin — basal body temp

Notes:

**THURSDAY** — cycle day — vitamin — basal body temp

Notes:

**FRIDAY** — cycle day — vitamin — basal body temp

Notes:

# looking ahead to pregnancy: morning sickness/nausea

Not long after your positive pregnancy test you may have another sign that you're pregnant. So-called morning sickness—nausea that can actually occur at any time of the day or night—affects more than three-quarters of pregnant women. Quell the queasiness by getting plenty of sleep, eating small meals five or six times a day (rather than three large meals), avoiding unpleasant odors, and wearing loose-fitting clothing. If your nausea is so severe it's getting in the way of good nutrition, ask your obstetrician for advice.

**SATURDAY** — cycle day — vitamin — basal body temp

Notes:

**SUNDAY** — cycle day — vitamin — basal body temp

Notes:

Think of five things you love to eat that are high in carbs or made from refined flours and sugars (like white breads, cereals, and sugary snacks). Now think of healthier, whole grain foods you can substitute for these items: for instance, choosing brown rice instead of white.

| Current Food | Substitute |
|---|---|
| | |
| | |
| | |
| | |
| | |

# month 3

# Vitamins and Nutritional Supplements

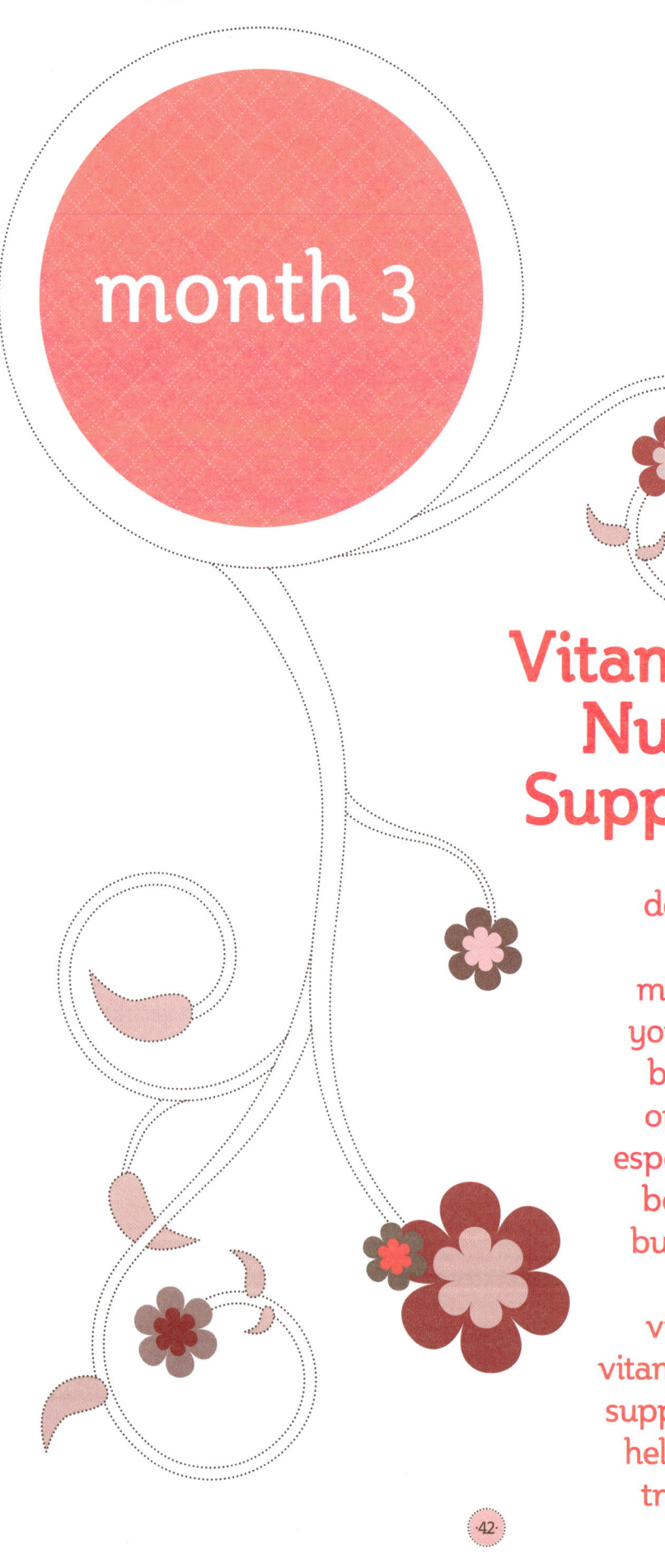

Even if you're doing your best to eat healthy, you might want to give your body an extra boost. Folic acid is one nutrient that's especially important before pregnancy, but it's not the only one. One-a-day vitamins, prenatal vitamins, and fertility supplements may be helpful while you're trying to conceive.

Did you begin taking a prenatal vitamin
at least 3 months before you started trying?     ○ Yes     ○ No

If so, what is its brand and name?..................................................................................

Does it contain at least 400 milligrams of folic acid?     ○ Yes     ○ No

Are there nutritional holes in your diet that could be filled in with supplements?..........
..............................................................................................................................
..............................................................................................................................

Are there any healthy foods or food groups that you dislike, so that your
diet doesn't contain the recommended amounts? (For instance, if you don't
like milk or dairy products, you may not be getting enough calcium every day.)
..............................................................................................................................
..............................................................................................................................

Are you a vegetarian or vegan?     ○ Yes     ○ No
..............................................................................................................................

If so, do you think you are consuming enough protein?.................................................
..............................................................................................................................

List any other nutritional supplements you take, including herbal preparations:
..............................................................................................................................
..............................................................................................................................

Have you asked your doctor whether
these will be safe to take while you're pregnant?     ○ Yes     ○ No

Would you consider taking a special supplement that promotes fertility?..................
..............................................................................................................................

# month 3
## week 1

### MONDAY ( ) cycle day ( ) vitamin ( ) basal body temp
Notes:

### TUESDAY ( ) cycle day ( ) vitamin ( ) basal body temp
Notes:

### WEDNESDAY ( ) cycle day ( ) vitamin ( ) basal body temp
Notes:

It's important to eat a rainbow of fruits and veggies to ensure a variety of important vitamins and nutrients. List your favorite fruits and vegetables by color:

| Red | Orange | Yellow | Green |
|-----|--------|--------|-------|
|     |        |        |       |
|     |        |        |       |
|     |        |        |       |
|     |        |        |       |
|     |        |        |       |
|     |        |        |       |
|     |        |        |       |

## assess what your body needs

Perhaps you turn up your nose at vegetables (many are high in folic acid), or get nauseated at the idea of a glass of milk (high in calcium). Maybe you think eating meat (high in iron) is cruel. If your current diet doesn't include a wide selection of grains, fruits, vegetables, and protein sources, you may be getting by for now, but need some help to boost your health and fertility for conception. Folic acid, iron, and calcium are the three of the most important nutrients for pregnancy prep, but there are others. Unless your diet would make a nutritionist proud, think about taking a daily vitamin to fill in the gaps.

# looking ahead to pregnancy: calcium

Women of reproductive age need about 1,000 milligrams of calcium a day, and pregnant women are advised to consume 1,200 milligrams. You'd need to consume a quarter pound of cheese, or four cups of milk or yogurt, or a pound of canned salmon (with bones) to get this amount. Your developing baby needs this calcium for strong bones and teeth, as well as proper nerve and muscle development. If a mom-to-be doesn't consume enough calcium during pregnancy, the mineral will be leached out of her own bones to nourish the baby. So be sure to take a calcium supplement if you don't get enough in your diet.

### THURSDAY ◦ cycle day ◦ vitamin ◦ basal body temp
Notes:

### FRIDAY ◦ cycle day ◦ vitamin ◦ basal body temp
Notes:

### SATURDAY ◦ cycle day ◦ vitamin ◦ basal body temp
Notes:

### SUNDAY ◦ cycle day ◦ vitamin ◦ basal body temp
Notes:

# month 3
## week 2

**MONDAY** — cycle day — vitamin — basal body temp

Notes:

**TUESDAY** — cycle day — vitamin — basal body temp

Notes:

**WEDNESDAY** — cycle day — vitamin — basal body temp

Notes:

## one-a-day vitamins

Many women have reasonably healthy diets and take a daily one-a-day-type vitamin each morning. The combination of healthy food and vitamin supplements is generally fine for conception. But not all vitamins are created equal. Make sure that whatever vitamin you choose contains at least 400 micrograms a day of folic acid, plus calcium and iron (especially if your diet isn't high in foods rich in these nutrients).

**THURSDAY** — cycle day — vitamin — basal body temp

Notes:

## looking ahead to pregnancy: iron

Research suggests that getting adequate iron during pregnancy may help prevent miscarriage. Iron is found in red meats, spinach, and fortified cereals, but your doctor may urge you to take a supplement, too.

**FRIDAY**   ⬚ cycle day   ⬚ vitamin   ⬚ basal body temp

Notes:

**SATURDAY**   ⬚ cycle day   ⬚ vitamin   ⬚ basal body temp

Notes:

**SUNDAY**   ⬚ cycle day   ⬚ vitamin   ⬚ basal body temp

Notes:

Are you taking a daily vitamin now?   yes   no

Have your needs changed since you began taking it?

How much folic acid is in your vitamin?

# month 3
## week 3

**MONDAY** ☐ cycle day ☐ vitamin ☐ basal body temp

Notes:

**TUESDAY** ☐ cycle day ☐ vitamin ☐ basal body temp

Notes:

**WEDNESDAY** ☐ cycle day ☐ vitamin ☐ basal body temp

Notes:

**THURSDAY** ☐ cycle day ☐ vitamin ☐ basal body temp

Notes:

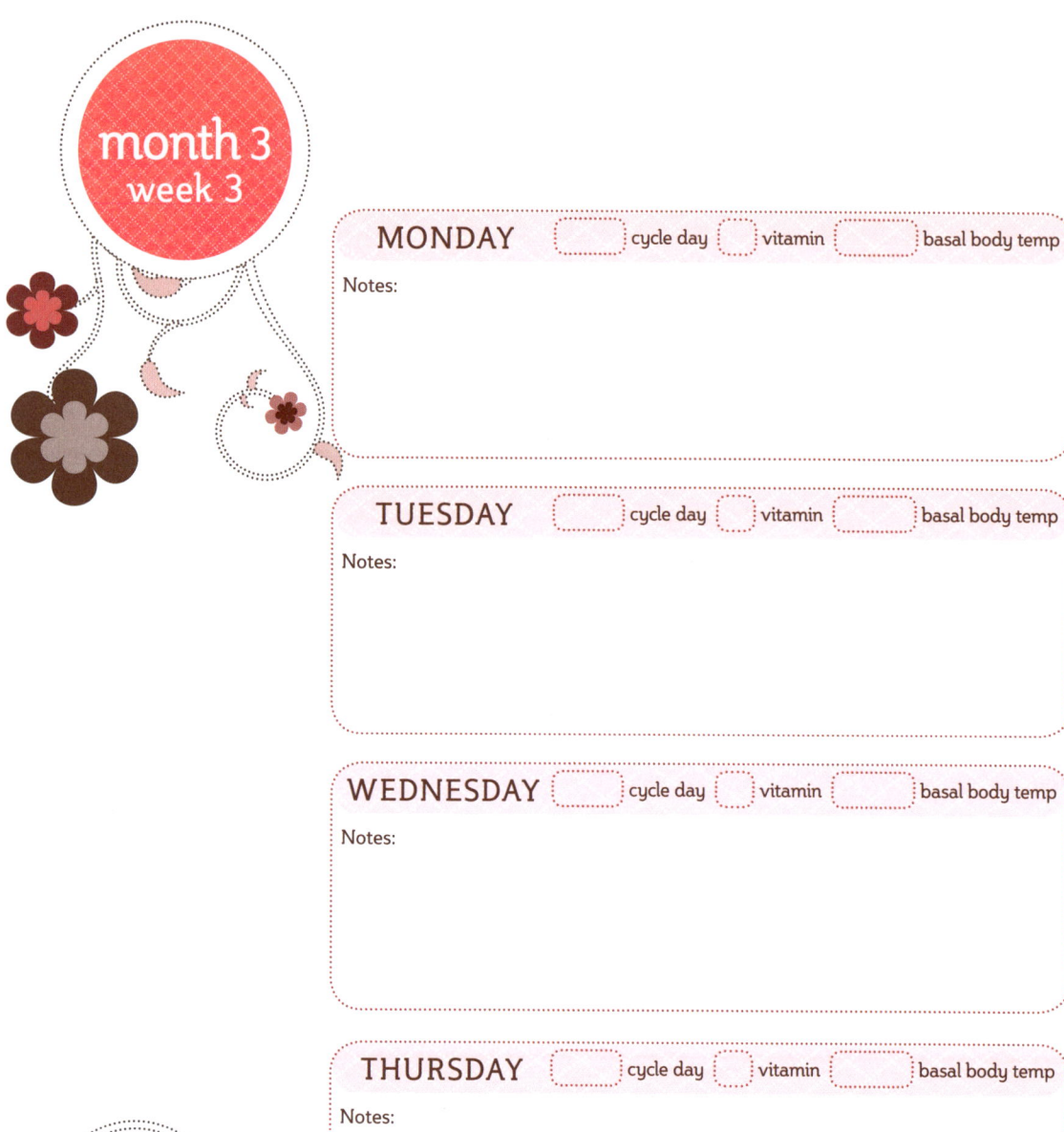

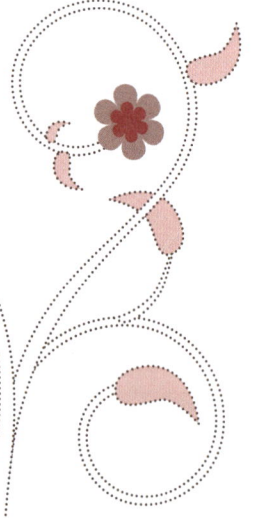

## looking ahead to pregnancy: prenatal vitamins

Once you're pregnant, prenatal vitamins aren't really optional. Nearly all obstetricians prescribe them so that nothing is left to chance when it comes to providing essential vitamins and minerals to your developing baby. If you began taking them before you were pregnant, you've got a great head start.

**FRIDAY**  ☐ cycle day  ☐ vitamin  ☐ basal body temp

Notes:

**SATURDAY**  ☐ cycle day  ☐ vitamin  ☐ basal body temp

Notes:

**SUNDAY**  ☐ cycle day  ☐ vitamin  ☐ basal body temp

Notes:

Most prenatal vitamins are different combinations of what your baby will need for healthy development, and they come in all shapes, sizes, and strengths. What are some things that you find most important when selecting a vitamin?

.................................................................................

.................................................................................

.................................................................................

.................................................................................

## prenatal vitamins before you're pregnant

Some doctors recommend that women begin taking prenatal vitamins as soon as they start trying to conceive. And now that there are prenatal vitamin formulas available without a prescription, some women simply decide to take them on their own. One nonfertility bonus to these vitamins: There are women who swear that the folic acid and biotin (a B-complex vitamin) make their hair and nails gorgeous!

# month 3
## week 4

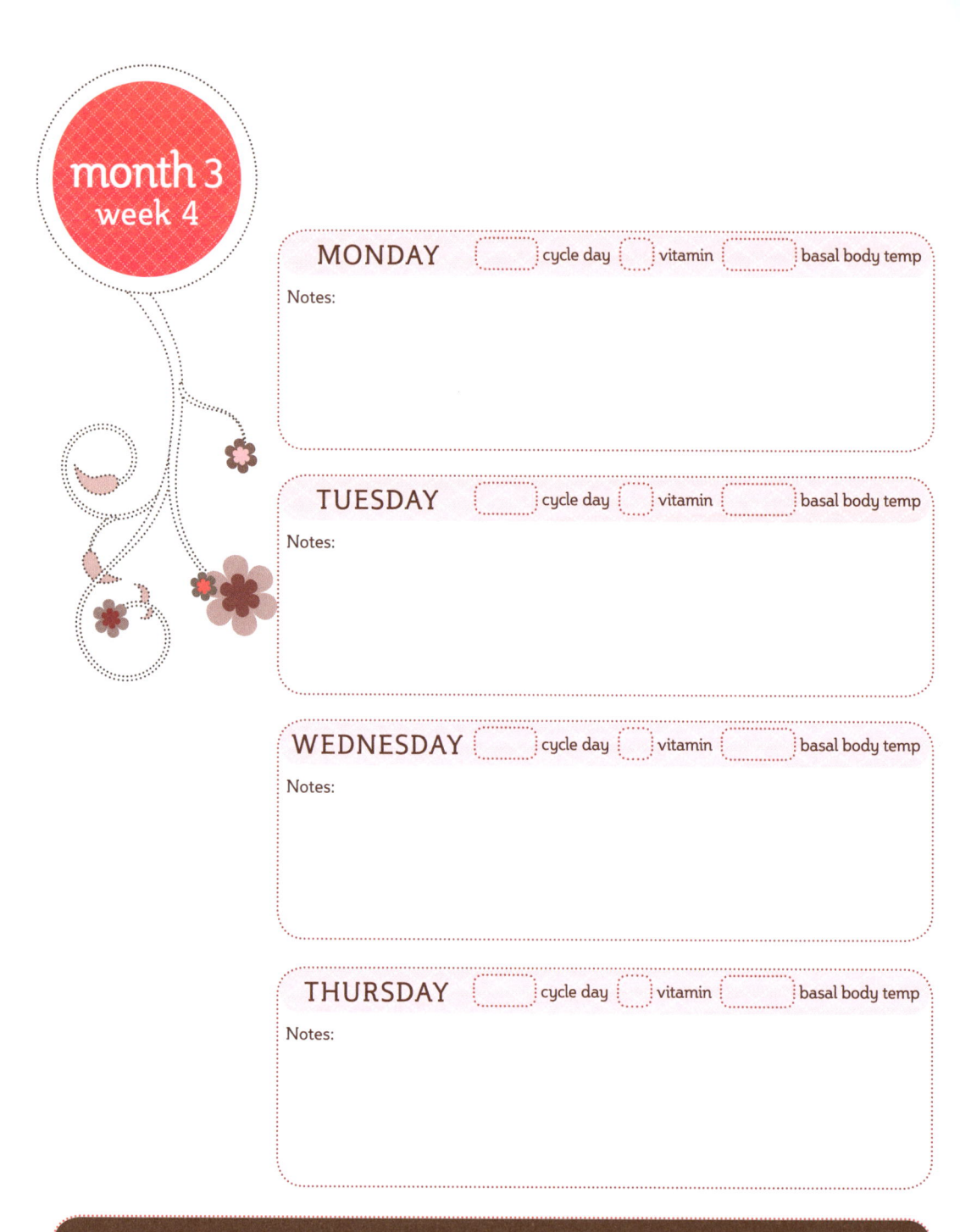

**MONDAY** ⬜ cycle day ⬜ vitamin ⬜ basal body temp
Notes:

**TUESDAY** ⬜ cycle day ⬜ vitamin ⬜ basal body temp
Notes:

**WEDNESDAY** ⬜ cycle day ⬜ vitamin ⬜ basal body temp
Notes:

**THURSDAY** ⬜ cycle day ⬜ vitamin ⬜ basal body temp
Notes:

## looking ahead to pregnancy: keeping those prenatal vitamins down

The majority of women suffer from some degree of so-called morning sickness (although it can happen at any time of the day) during pregnancy. Even swallowing a vitamin pill might make you gag, or even vomit. If you find you have trouble keeping your prenatal vitamins down, ask your doctor to recommend a liquid or chewable version that's easier to swallow.

## nutritional supplements

Many women planning to get pregnant take nutritional supplements in addition to their prenatal or one-a-day-type vitamins. These supplements may be additional nutrients (such as calcium, iron, or omega-3 oils), special fertility preparations or other herbal products. Whatever you're taking, let your doctor know to make sure that it's safe while you're trying to conceive.

**FRIDAY**   ( ) cycle day   ( ) vitamin   ( ) basal body temp

Notes:

**SATURDAY**   ( ) cycle day   ( ) vitamin   ( ) basal body temp

Notes:

**SUNDAY**   ( ) cycle day   ( ) vitamin   ( ) basal body temp

Notes:

Now that you've tracked three of your cycles . . .

What have you learned about your cycle so far?

..................................................................................................................

Is your cycle fairly regular? About how many days?

..................................................................................................................

When do you ovulate each cycle? ...............................................................

# month 4

## Kick the Habit

Everyone has a few bad habits, whether it's biting your nails, twirling your hair, or eating too much chocolate. But some bad habits are more than just annoying or calorie-laden: some can affect your goal of conceiving and having a healthy pregnancy. Bite your nails if you must, but find out which habits you'll need to get under control now.

What are your worst habits? ............................................................................................
..................................................................................................................................
..................................................................................................................................

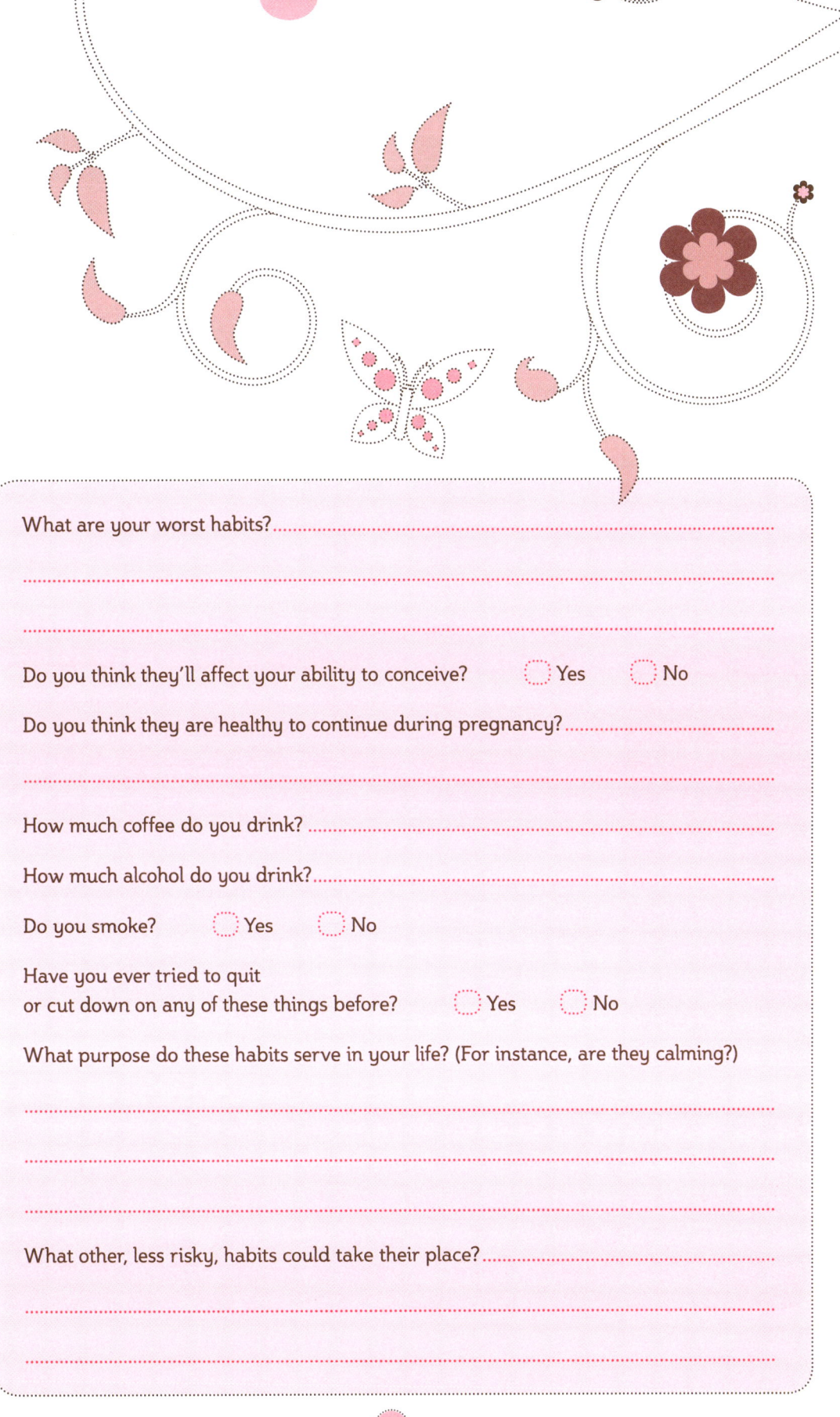

Do you think they'll affect your ability to conceive?   ◯ Yes   ◯ No

Do you think they are healthy to continue during pregnancy? ..........................................
..................................................................................................................................

How much coffee do you drink? ....................................................................................

How much alcohol do you drink? ..................................................................................

Do you smoke?   ◯ Yes   ◯ No

Have you ever tried to quit
or cut down on any of these things before?   ◯ Yes   ◯ No

What purpose do these habits serve in your life? (For instance, are they calming?)
..................................................................................................................................
..................................................................................................................................
..................................................................................................................................

What other, less risky, habits could take their place? ....................................................
..................................................................................................................................
..................................................................................................................................

# month 4
## week 1

**MONDAY** — cycle day — vitamin — basal body temp
Notes:

**TUESDAY** — cycle day — vitamin — basal body temp
Notes:

**WEDNESDAY** — cycle day — vitamin — basal body temp
Notes:

**THURSDAY** — cycle day — vitamin — basal body temp
Notes:

## smoking

Smoking is unhealthy when you're not trying to conceive, but its harmful effects increase when you're trying to get pregnant. Smoking affects estrogen levels, cervical mucus, and the supply of eggs in the ovaries, lowering fertility.

## looking ahead to pregnancy: no more excuses!

Once you're pregnant, your smoking becomes a risk to the developing child inside you. Women who smoke are at increased risk of having a miscarriage, placental problems, preterm delivery, and a low birthweight baby.

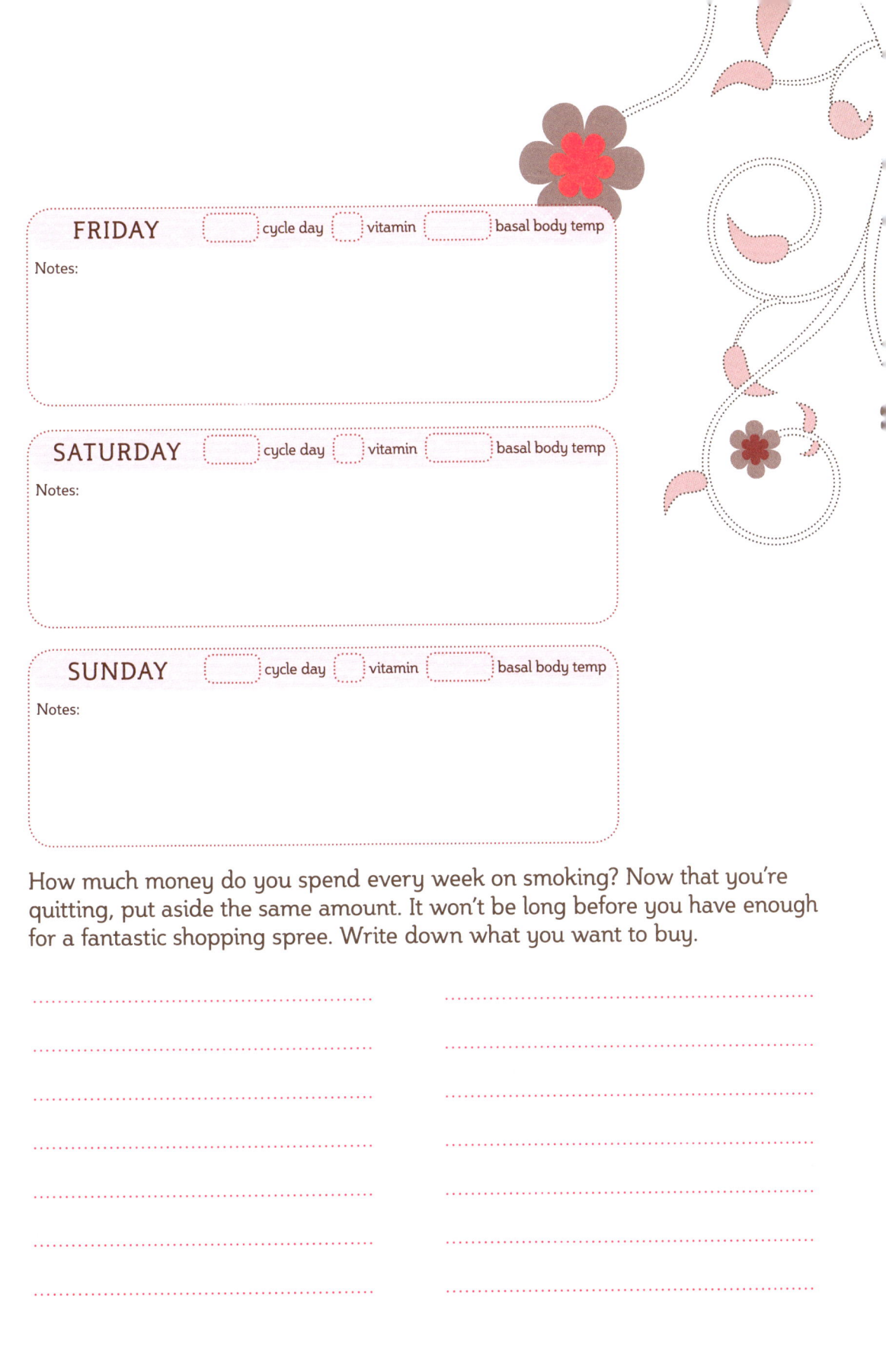

### FRIDAY　　cycle day　　vitamin　　basal body temp
Notes:

### SATURDAY　　cycle day　　vitamin　　basal body temp
Notes:

### SUNDAY　　cycle day　　vitamin　　basal body temp
Notes:

How much money do you spend every week on smoking? Now that you're quitting, put aside the same amount. It won't be long before you have enough for a fantastic shopping spree. Write down what you want to buy.

# month 4
## week 2

### MONDAY  cycle day  vitamin  basal body temp
Notes:

### TUESDAY  cycle day  vitamin  basal body temp
Notes:

### WEDNESDAY  cycle day  vitamin  basal body temp
Notes:

### THURSDAY  cycle day  vitamin  basal body temp
Notes:

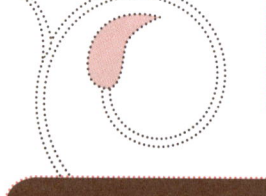

## looking ahead to pregnancy: zero alcohol

Heavy drinking is a well-known pregnancy risk factor and can lead to serious abnormalities in newborns. But experts say that there's no data to show what a safe level of alcohol consumption during pregnancy is, so they advise pregnant women to avoid alcohol completely. Once your baby is born you can toast the birth with champagne, but until then, abstain!

What's your favorite nonalcoholic drink? Do you like decaf lattes? Cola with lime? Virgin coladas? Write down your favorite "mocktail" recipe here, and serve it at your next dinner party. Or ask a pregnant friend for her favorites.

..........................................................................................................................
..........................................................................................................................
..........................................................................................................................
..........................................................................................................................
..........................................................................................................................

**FRIDAY** — cycle day — vitamin — basal body temp

Notes:

**SATURDAY** — cycle day — vitamin — basal body temp

Notes:

**SUNDAY** — cycle day — vitamin — basal body temp

Notes:

## all about alcohol

Doctors generally agree that moderate drinking is okay when you're trying to conceive, but once you're pregnant you need to abstain completely. If you're more than an occasional drinker, now is a good time to get this habit under control. Otherwise you might have difficulty going "cold turkey" once you get that positive pregnancy test.

# month 4 week 3

**MONDAY** ( ) cycle day ( ) vitamin ( ) basal body temp
Notes:

**TUESDAY** ( ) cycle day ( ) vitamin ( ) basal body temp
Notes:

**WEDNESDAY** ( ) cycle day ( ) vitamin ( ) basal body temp
Notes:

**THURSDAY** ( ) cycle day ( ) vitamin ( ) basal body temp
Notes:

**FRIDAY** ( ) cycle day ( ) vitamin ( ) basal body temp
Notes:

---

## joe or no joe?

Caffeine's role in fertility and pregnancy is still not well understood. Research results have been conflicting, and the verdict is still out. Most doctors agree that as long as you limit your intake to the equivalent of two or three small caffeinated drinks a day, you should be okay. But if you're on a first name basis with your local barista, you might want to cut back.

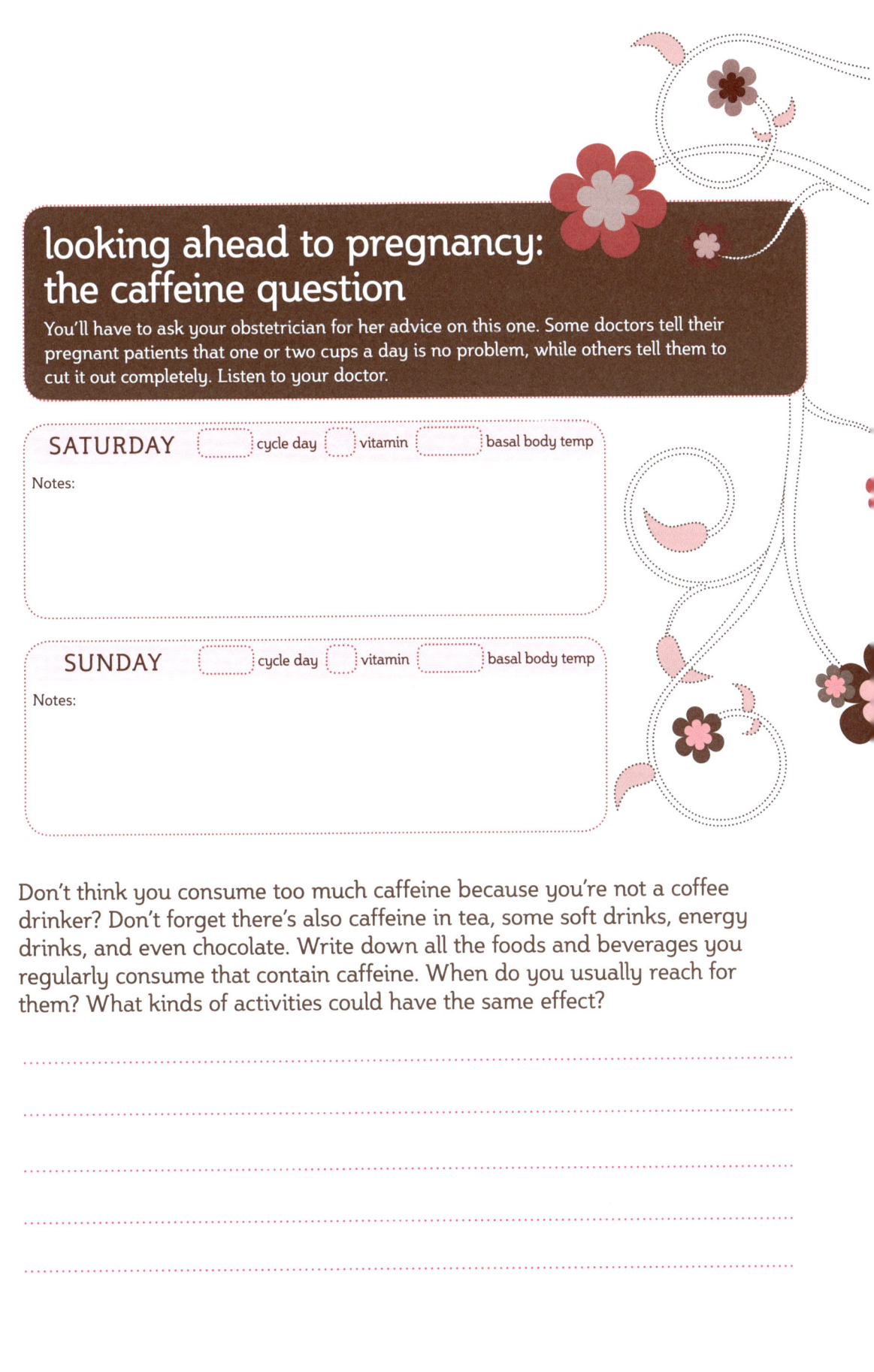

# looking ahead to pregnancy: the caffeine question

You'll have to ask your obstetrician for her advice on this one. Some doctors tell their pregnant patients that one or two cups a day is no problem, while others tell them to cut it out completely. Listen to your doctor.

**SATURDAY** ⬜ cycle day ⬜ vitamin ⬜ basal body temp

Notes:

**SUNDAY** ⬜ cycle day ⬜ vitamin ⬜ basal body temp

Notes:

Don't think you consume too much caffeine because you're not a coffee drinker? Don't forget there's also caffeine in tea, some soft drinks, energy drinks, and even chocolate. Write down all the foods and beverages you regularly consume that contain caffeine. When do you usually reach for them? What kinds of activities could have the same effect?

..........................................................................................................................

..........................................................................................................................

..........................................................................................................................

..........................................................................................................................

..........................................................................................................................

## month 4
### week 4

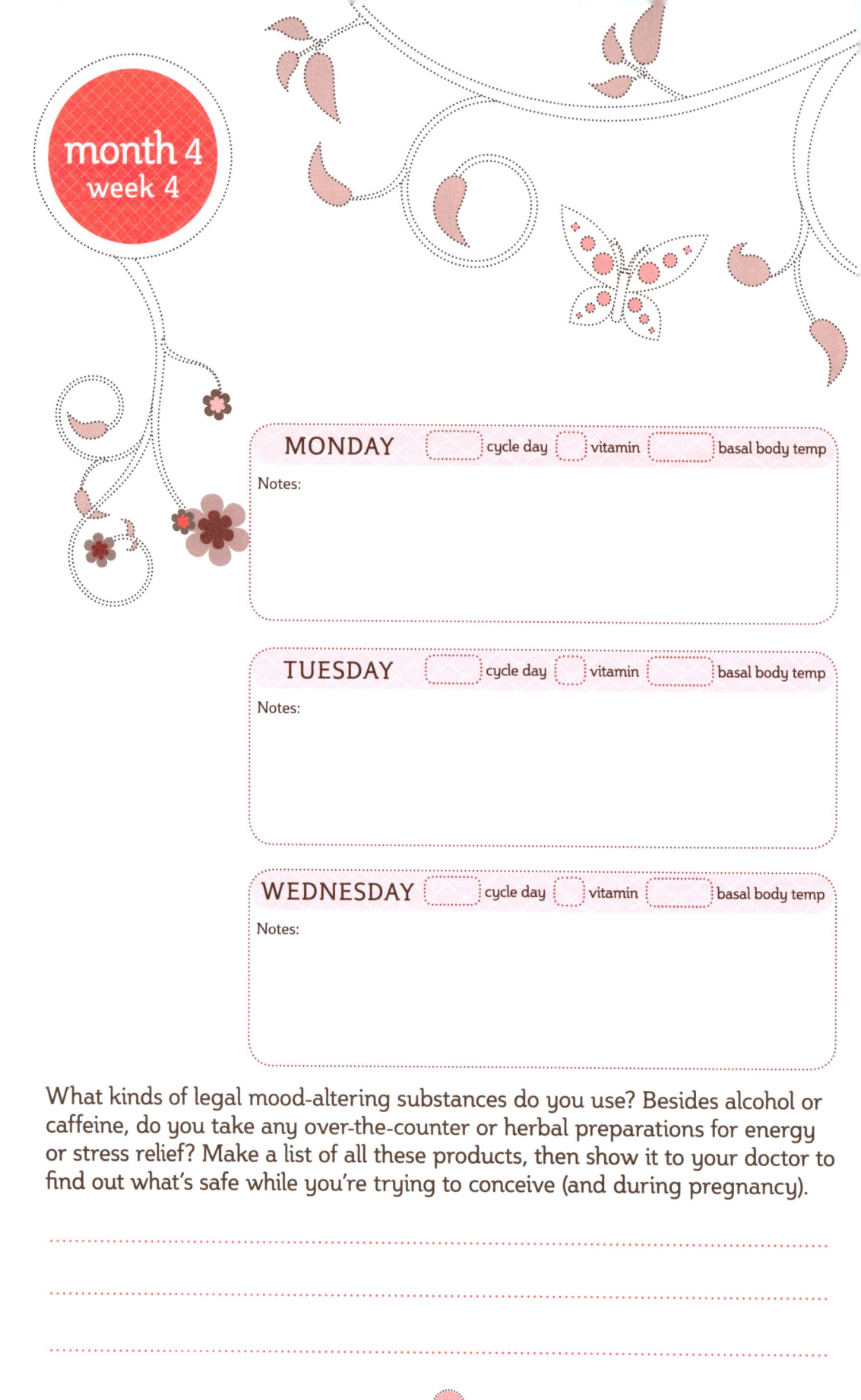

**MONDAY** — cycle day — vitamin — basal body temp
Notes:

**TUESDAY** — cycle day — vitamin — basal body temp
Notes:

**WEDNESDAY** — cycle day — vitamin — basal body temp
Notes:

What kinds of legal mood-altering substances do you use? Besides alcohol or caffeine, do you take any over-the-counter or herbal preparations for energy or stress relief? Make a list of all these products, then show it to your doctor to find out what's safe while you're trying to conceive (and during pregnancy).

# looking ahead to pregnancy: the law

Babies born to addicted mothers can suffer horrendous health problems that last throughout life. And women who use illegal drugs during pregnancy may be subject to especially harsh legal penalties. Again, no room for moderation. If you're still using drugs when you become pregnant, seek help right away.

### THURSDAY ⬚ cycle day ⬚ vitamin ⬚ basal body temp
Notes:

### FRIDAY ⬚ cycle day ⬚ vitamin ⬚ basal body temp
Notes:

### SATURDAY ⬚ cycle day ⬚ vitamin ⬚ basal body temp
Notes:

### SUNDAY ⬚ cycle day ⬚ vitamin ⬚ basal body temp
Notes:

## just say no

No room for moderation here. Not only are marijuana, cocaine, and other recreational drugs illegal, but they're also a fertility and pregnancy risk. These drugs can interfere with ovulation, or block sperm from reaching the egg. Quit or seek help—immediately.

# month 5

## Weighting for Pregnancy

You might anticipate that you're going to get obsessed about your weight during pregnancy—How much should you gain? How quickly will you lose it afterward?—but you may not realize how important it is to consider what you weigh NOW. Being too thin or too heavy can make it hard—or even impossible—to conceive. Get the skinny on the right size for maximum fertility.

What is your weight history? ............................................................................................
..........................................................................................................................................

Is your weight fairly steady, does it go up and
down a few pounds, or do you have huge gains and losses? ......................................
..........................................................................................................................................
..........................................................................................................................................

If you've battled your weight for much of your life, what are you unhappy with?
..........................................................................................................................................
..........................................................................................................................................

Do you wish you were a different size for fashion . . . or for health? ..........................
..........................................................................................................................................

Have you ever been on a diet? .......................................................................................
Are you a fad dieter? Low- or no-carb dieter? Liquid dieter? ......................................
..........................................................................................................................................

Were these efforts successful?    ◯ Yes    ◯ No
If so, what helped motivate you and ensure your success? ........................................
..........................................................................................................................................

How long were you able to keep the weight off? ..........................................................
Do you feel you need to lose or gain more than 5 or 10 pounds?    ◯ Yes    ◯ No
What would motivate you to lose or gain weight now? ................................................
..........................................................................................................................................
..........................................................................................................................................
..........................................................................................................................................

## month 5
### week 1

**MONDAY** ☐ cycle day ☐ vitamin ☐ basal body temp
Notes:

**TUESDAY** ☐ cycle day ☐ vitamin ☐ basal body temp
Notes:

**WEDNESDAY** ☐ cycle day ☐ vitamin ☐ basal body temp
Notes:

**THURSDAY** ☐ cycle day ☐ vitamin ☐ basal body temp
Notes:

## looking ahead to pregnancy: how much weight should you gain?

How much weight should you gain when you're pregnant? The answer might surprise you. Most doctors recommend that women who begin their pregnancy at a healthy BMI gain between 25 and 35 pounds (although lately physicians have been urging women to stay at the lower end of this scale). Women who are overweight when they conceive may be advised to keep their weight gain to around 15 pounds, while severely underweight women may be told they need to gain even more than 35. Your obstetrician will tell you what's right for you.

# learn your body mass index (BMI)

Your body mass index is a measure of body fat calculated using your height and weight:

$$\frac{\text{Weight in pounds}}{(\text{Height in inches})^2} \times 703 = \text{BMI}$$

A normal, healthy BMI is between 18.5 and 24.9. You're considered underweight if your BMI is below 18.5. Overweight is 25 to 29.9, and obese is 30 or higher. A normal, healthy BMI—between 18.5 and 24.9—is also the most fertile.

**FRIDAY** ⬚ cycle day ⬚ vitamin ⬚ basal body temp

Notes:

**SATURDAY** ⬚ cycle day ⬚ vitamin ⬚ basal body temp

Notes:

**SUNDAY** ⬚ cycle day ⬚ vitamin ⬚ basal body temp

Notes:

Calculate your BMI

$$\frac{\text{_____ lbs.}}{(\text{height in inches})^2} \times 703$$

Your BMI is

If your BMI is not between 18.5 and 24.9, list a few simple changes you can make to safely lose—or gain—a few pounds before pregnancy.

## month 5
### week 2

**MONDAY** — cycle day — vitamin — basal body temp
Notes:

**TUESDAY** — cycle day — vitamin — basal body temp
Notes:

**WEDNESDAY** — cycle day — vitamin — basal body temp
Notes:

## lose a little (weight), gain a lot (pregnancy)

If you're too heavy, losing as little as 5 to 10 percent of your body weight, or as little as 10 pounds, can make a difference in your efforts to conceive. Body fat produces a weak form of estrogen, and when women have too much body fat, the brain can be fooled into thinking that the hormones are all doing their jobs. The result is that the egg release cycle may not occur. Lose some of the fat and the balance may tip back toward normal ovulation.

| What are your biggest challenges when it comes to eating well? | Are those barriers still in place now? |
|---|---|
| ................................................................ | yes  no |
| ................................................................ | yes  no |
| ................................................................ | yes  no |
| ................................................................ | yes  no |

# looking ahead to pregnancy: first trimester weight gain

Even though a pregnancy lasts nine months, weight gain isn't distributed evenly over this time. Ideally, women should gain only about four pounds during the first trimester, another 10 to 12 during the second trimester, and the remaining 10 to 20 pounds after that.

## THURSDAY     cycle day     vitamin     basal body temp
Notes:

## FRIDAY     cycle day     vitamin     basal body temp
Notes:

## SATURDAY     cycle day     vitamin     basal body temp
Notes:

## SUNDAY     cycle day     vitamin     basal body temp
Notes:

# month 5
## week 3

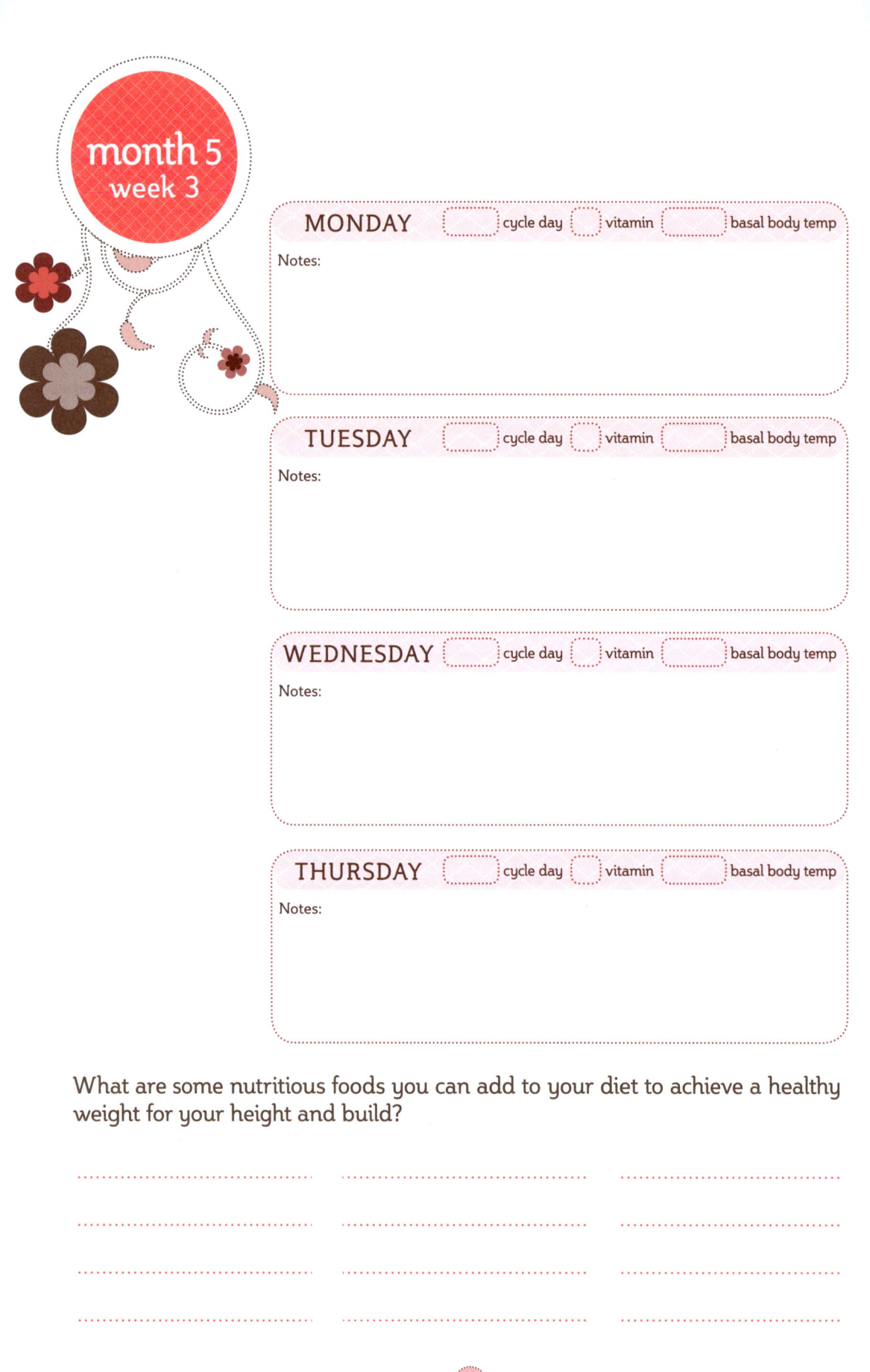

**MONDAY** — cycle day — vitamin — basal body temp
Notes:

**TUESDAY** — cycle day — vitamin — basal body temp
Notes:

**WEDNESDAY** — cycle day — vitamin — basal body temp
Notes:

**THURSDAY** — cycle day — vitamin — basal body temp
Notes:

What are some nutritious foods you can add to your diet to achieve a healthy weight for your height and build?

# gain a little (weight), gain a lot (pregnancy)

If you're too thin, gaining as few as five pounds can make the difference between getting pregnant or not. When levels of body fat are low, the hypothalamus, the brain's hormone command center, receives a signal that there's too little body fat—and too little estrogen—to support a pregnancy. To prevent a pregnancy from occurring, the brain doesn't signal the pituitary gland to release the hormones necessary for ovulation. Again, just a small change in weight—in this case, a slight gain—can often restore hormonal balance.

### FRIDAY
cycle day ___ vitamin ___ basal body temp ___
Notes:

### SATURDAY
cycle day ___ vitamin ___ basal body temp ___
Notes:

### SUNDAY
cycle day ___ vitamin ___ basal body temp ___
Notes:

# looking ahead to pregnancy: weight gain isn't fat gain

You might wonder why you're supposed to gain twenty-five or thirty-five pounds when your baby will probably only weigh seven or eight. Fat only makes up some of the extra weight. The rest is distributed between blood, breasts, uterus, placenta, amniotic fluid, protein and other nutrients, and retained water.

# month 5
## week 4

**MONDAY** ⬚ cycle day ⬚ vitamin ⬚ basal body temp
Notes:

**TUESDAY** ⬚ cycle day ⬚ vitamin ⬚ basal body temp
Notes:

**WEDNESDAY** ⬚ cycle day ⬚ vitamin ⬚ basal body temp
Notes:

**THURSDAY** ⬚ cycle day ⬚ vitamin ⬚ basal body temp
Notes:

## slow and steady

If you've decided you're going to aim for a healthy weight—and healthy BMI—while you're trying to conceive, it's especially important that you take it slow and healthy. Now is not the time for fad diets of any kind. Instead of cutting your calorie intake drastically or completely eliminating food groups from your diet, take a more measured approach. Programs such as Weight Watchers can help you lose weight sensibly.

## looking ahead to pregnancy: getting your body back

Many women follow their doctors' advice about gaining weight during pregnancy, but worry throughout the nine months that they'll never be able to lose the extra weight. But if you eat healthy during pregnancy and don't gain more than the recommended amount, chances are you'll be back at your prepregnancy weight—or very close to it—in just a few months.

### FRIDAY ⬚ cycle day ⬚ vitamin ⬚ basal body temp
Notes:

### SATURDAY ⬚ cycle day ⬚ vitamin ⬚ basal body temp
Notes:

### SUNDAY ⬚ cycle day ⬚ vitamin ⬚ basal body temp
Notes:

| List all of the diets you have tried, whether they're named after a person, a place, or a thing. | Did it work? | Did you gain the weight back? |
|---|---|---|
| ............................................................................... | yes  no | yes  no |
| ............................................................................... | yes  no | yes  no |
| ............................................................................... | yes  no | yes  no |
| ............................................................................... | yes  no | yes  no |
| ............................................................................... | yes  no | yes  no |
| ............................................................................... | yes  no | yes  no |
| ............................................................................... | yes  no | yes  no |
| ............................................................................... | yes  no | yes  no |
| ............................................................................... | yes  no | yes  no |

# month 6

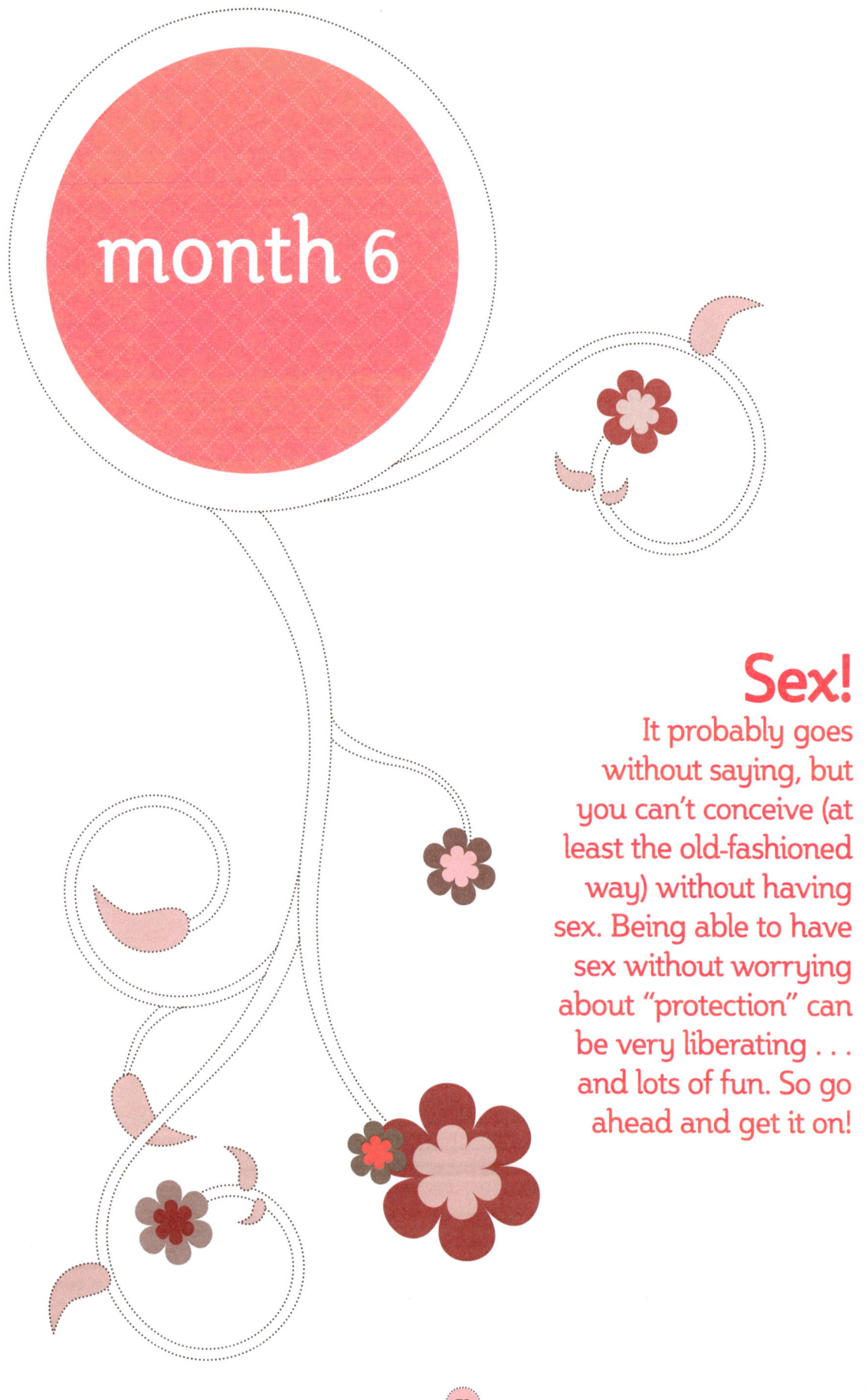

## Sex!

It probably goes without saying, but you can't conceive (at least the old-fashioned way) without having sex. Being able to have sex without worrying about "protection" can be very liberating . . . and lots of fun. So go ahead and get it on!

How often do you and your husband or partner usually have sex?

What do you love most about having sex?

What's the most exciting sex you've ever had?

The most romantic sex you've ever had?

What kind of contraceptives are/were you using?

How does the idea of having "unprotected" sex make you feel?

Are there any sexual problems in your relationship that should be addressed now?

# month 6
## week 1

**MONDAY** ⬚ cycle day ⬚ vitamin ⬚ basal body temp

Notes:

**TUESDAY** ⬚ cycle day ⬚ vitamin ⬚ basal body temp

Notes:

**WEDNESDAY** ⬚ cycle day ⬚ vitamin ⬚ basal body temp

Notes:

**THURSDAY** ⬚ cycle day ⬚ vitamin ⬚ basal body temp

Notes:

**FRIDAY** ⬚ cycle day ⬚ vitamin ⬚ basal body temp

Notes:

## when to have sex

Determining when you're most fertile—around the time of ovulation—is the most important factor in successful procreation sex. Read (or reread) the section about ovulation at the beginning of this journal. Knowing your cycle is the single best thing you can do for success.

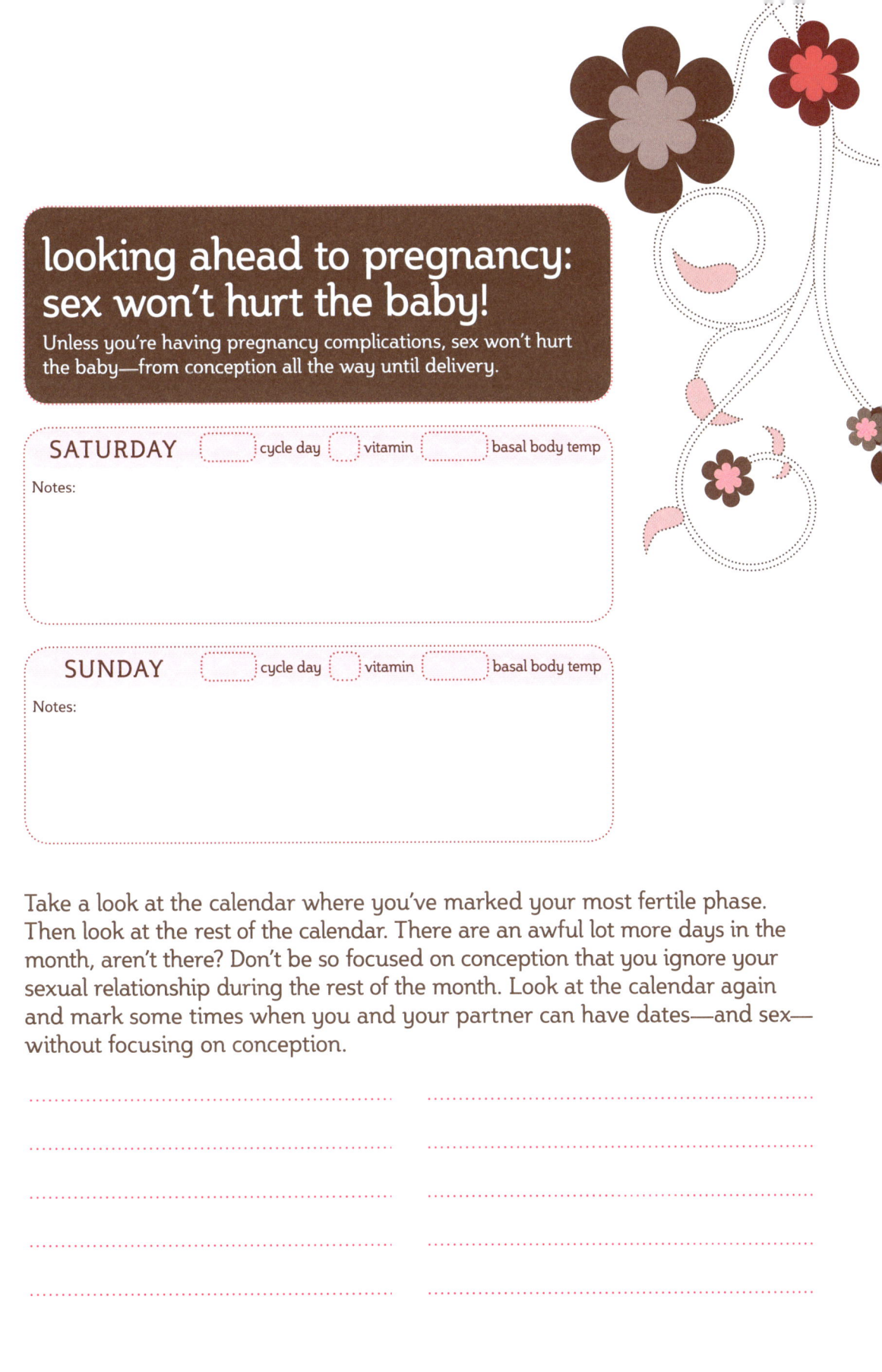

## looking ahead to pregnancy: sex won't hurt the baby!

Unless you're having pregnancy complications, sex won't hurt the baby—from conception all the way until delivery.

**SATURDAY** ⬚ cycle day ⬚ vitamin ⬚ basal body temp

Notes:

**SUNDAY** ⬚ cycle day ⬚ vitamin ⬚ basal body temp

Notes:

Take a look at the calendar where you've marked your most fertile phase. Then look at the rest of the calendar. There are an awful lot more days in the month, aren't there? Don't be so focused on conception that you ignore your sexual relationship during the rest of the month. Look at the calendar again and mark some times when you and your partner can have dates—and sex—without focusing on conception.

# month 6
## week 2

**MONDAY** — cycle day — vitamin — basal body temp
Notes:

**TUESDAY** — cycle day — vitamin — basal body temp
Notes:

**WEDNESDAY** — cycle day — vitamin — basal body temp
Notes:

There's obviously more to a good relationship than sex. Don't forget the romance, whether you're having sex to conceive or just for fun. Make a list of romantic things you can do for your partner. Now make one of things he can do for you. Then start checking them off . . .

### for you

- 
- 
- 
- 
- 
- 

### for him

- 
- 
- 
- 
- 
-

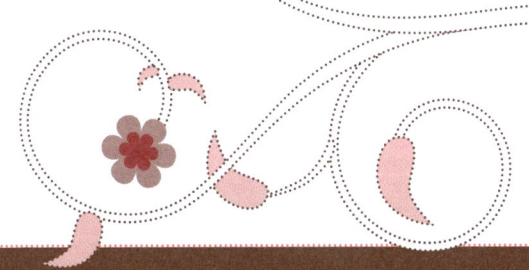

# looking ahead to pregnancy: your changing body

Some pregnant women worry that their burgeoning belly will turn their partner off, but most men find their partner extremely attractive during pregnancy. You might worry about the big bump, but your man is probably more focused on your bigger pregnancy breasts!

**THURSDAY** — cycle day — vitamin — basal body temp

Notes:

**FRIDAY** — cycle day — vitamin — basal body temp

Notes:

**SATURDAY** — cycle day — vitamin — basal body temp

Notes:

**SUNDAY** — cycle day — vitamin — basal body temp

Notes:

## how often should you have sex to conceive?

Once you've determined your most fertile days, you might think that having sex on each of those days—or even several times a day—will up your chances of success. Wrong. Most fertility experts recommend that couples have sex every other day starting about a week before ovulation. Since sperm can live in the female reproductive tract for a few days, having sex every other day will ensure that sperm are present when you ovulate. Too much sex can actually reduce a man's sperm count temporarily.

## month 6
### week 3

**MONDAY** ⬚ cycle day ⬚ vitamin ⬚ basal body temp
Notes:

**TUESDAY** ⬚ cycle day ⬚ vitamin ⬚ basal body temp
Notes:

**WEDNESDAY** ⬚ cycle day ⬚ vitamin ⬚ basal body temp
Notes:

Now that a few months have gone by, you and your partner may start to feel that sex has become a chore. Fight that feeling! What would make sex fun again? What always gets you in the mood?

# looking ahead to pregnancy: changing desires

Many women experience less interest in sex during the first trimester, which isn't surprising considering the fatigue and nausea so many women feel. But sexual desire usually perks up again during the second trimester, when nausea subsides and energy returns.

### THURSDAY   cycle day   vitamin   basal body temp
Notes:

### FRIDAY   cycle day   vitamin   basal body temp
Notes:

### SATURDAY   cycle day   vitamin   basal body temp
Notes:

### SUNDAY   cycle day   vitamin   basal body temp
Notes:

## assume the position

There is no conception *Kama Sutra*. There's also no need to restrict yourself to the missionary position. Conception can happen from any position. Do what's tried and true, or try something new.

## month 6
### week 4

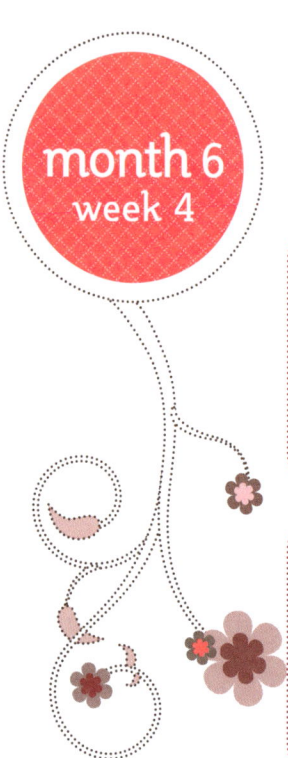

**MONDAY** ☐ cycle day ☐ vitamin ☐ basal body temp
Notes:

**TUESDAY** ☐ cycle day ☐ vitamin ☐ basal body temp
Notes:

**WEDNESDAY** ☐ cycle day ☐ vitamin ☐ basal body temp
Notes:

**THURSDAY** ☐ cycle day ☐ vitamin ☐ basal body temp
Notes:

## don't just lie there

Many women—and some doctors—think that lying in bed after sex, with legs up in the air and hips raised, will help the conception efforts. Don't bother. There's no evidence that sperm need any help in the gravity department. Lounge around in bed if you want to, but if you'd rather get up and do something, go right ahead.

## looking ahead to pregnancy: babymoons

Pregnancy is another great time for a couple's vacation. After all, soon you'll have a baby to take care of, and that might make romance and togetherness difficult, at least for a little while. Many resorts and hotels now offer special "babymoon" packages that include spa treatments for pregnant women and romantic dinners for couples.

**FRIDAY**  ◯ cycle day  ◯ vitamin  ◯ basal body temp

Notes:

**SATURDAY**  ◯ cycle day  ◯ vitamin  ◯ basal body temp

Notes:

**SUNDAY**  ◯ cycle day  ◯ vitamin  ◯ basal body temp

Notes:

So many couples have busy, stressful lives that make relaxing together—for sex or anything else—difficult. Taking a vacation together when you're trying to conceive can be surprisingly helpful. Make a list of places you'd like to visit, for a week, a weekend, or even a day. Then check the calendar and see when you can both take time off from work that will coincide with your fertile phase.

# month 7

## Fertility for Him

Women may be the stars of conception and pregnancy, but men play more than supporting roles. After all, it takes two to make a baby. And when problems occur, they're just as likely to be on the male side as on the female one. So show the following pages to your baby-making partner, and let him know that his role is an important one, too.

Overall, how healthy is your guy? ..................................................................
..........................................................................................................................

Are there any recurring health problems or issues that he's dealing with? ..................
..........................................................................................................................

How old is he? ....................................................................................................

Does he work out regularly?　　　◯ Yes　　◯ No

What kind of exercises does he do? ..................................................................
..........................................................................................................................
..........................................................................................................................

What are his unhealthy habits? ..........................................................................
..........................................................................................................................

Has he had a check-up recently?　　◯ Yes　　◯ No

Does he have children already? ..........................................................................
..........................................................................................................................

Is he exposed to chemicals that might affect his fertility? ..................................
..........................................................................................................................

## month 7
### week 1

**MONDAY** ( ) cycle day ( ) vitamin ( ) basal body temp
Notes:

**TUESDAY** ( ) cycle day ( ) vitamin ( ) basal body temp
Notes:

**WEDNESDAY** ( ) cycle day ( ) vitamin ( ) basal body temp
Notes:

**THURSDAY** ( ) cycle day ( ) vitamin ( ) basal body temp
Notes:

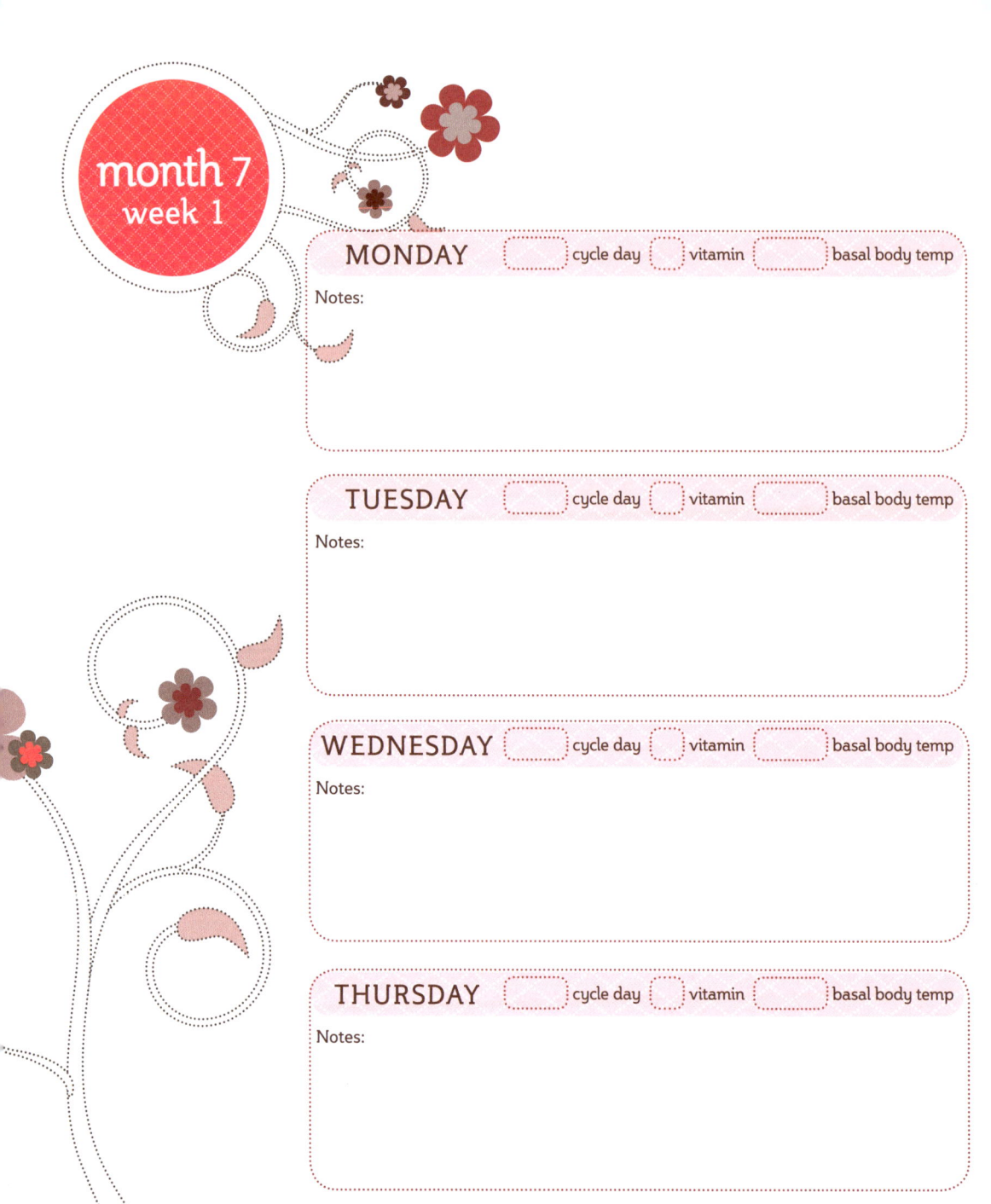

## looking ahead to pregnancy: the family diet

Once you're pregnant you'll want to be especially careful about what you eat, but your partner's diet may seem less important; his physical role in creating the pregnancy has ended. But a supportive partner will share your healthy diet to make it easier for you to get the nutrients you need. Also, sharing a nutritious diet as a couple will help you establish the pattern of healthy eating as a family, giving your children a head start on a lifetime of good nutrition.

**FRIDAY** — cycle day — vitamin — basal body temp

Notes:

**SATURDAY** — cycle day — vitamin — basal body temp

Notes:

**SUNDAY** — cycle day — vitamin — basal body temp

Notes:

## food for him

Good health is just as important for men who want to father a child as it is for women who are hoping to get pregnant. Two minerals that are important for sperm production are zinc and selenium. Zinc is found in oysters, beef, veal, lamb, pork, shellfish, wheat germ, wheat bran, and spinach. Selenium is in Brazil nuts, tuna, beef, cod, turkey, and chicken breast, enriched pastas, eggs, cottage cheese, and rice.

What are your man's favorite foods? What meals can you create out of the fertility-enhancing foods, listed above, that he'll love? Make a shopping list—and then send him out to the store!

# month 7
## week 2

**MONDAY** — cycle day — vitamin — basal body temp
Notes:

**TUESDAY** — cycle day — vitamin — basal body temp
Notes:

## the fertility workout for him

Exercise is important for male fertility, since it promotes general well-being and a healthy body weight. The three biggest concerns for hopeful daddies-to-be who want to work out are heat (see page 89), pressure (from bicycle seats, for instance), and trauma (from injury). Keep those private parts cool and well protected!

**WEDNESDAY** — cycle day — vitamin — basal body temp
Notes:

**THURSDAY** — cycle day — vitamin — basal body temp
Notes:

Calculate your man's BMI (body mass index) using the formula on page 65. Men who are significantly overweight or underweight can have lower sperm counts and sperm concentration.

**FRIDAY** ⬚ cycle day ⬚ vitamin ⬚ basal body temp

Notes:

**SATURDAY** ⬚ cycle day ⬚ vitamin ⬚ basal body temp

Notes:

## looking ahead to pregnancy: couples' exercise

Taking long walks with your partner or going to the gym can be another way to promote togetherness—and fitness—while you're pregnant. Set up a regular date for a long walk followed by lunch. Or stop at the gym after your childbirth education classes.

**SUNDAY** ⬚ cycle day ⬚ vitamin ⬚ basal body temp

Notes:

# month 7
## week 3

**MONDAY** ⬚ cycle day ⬚ vitamin ⬚ basal body temp
Notes:

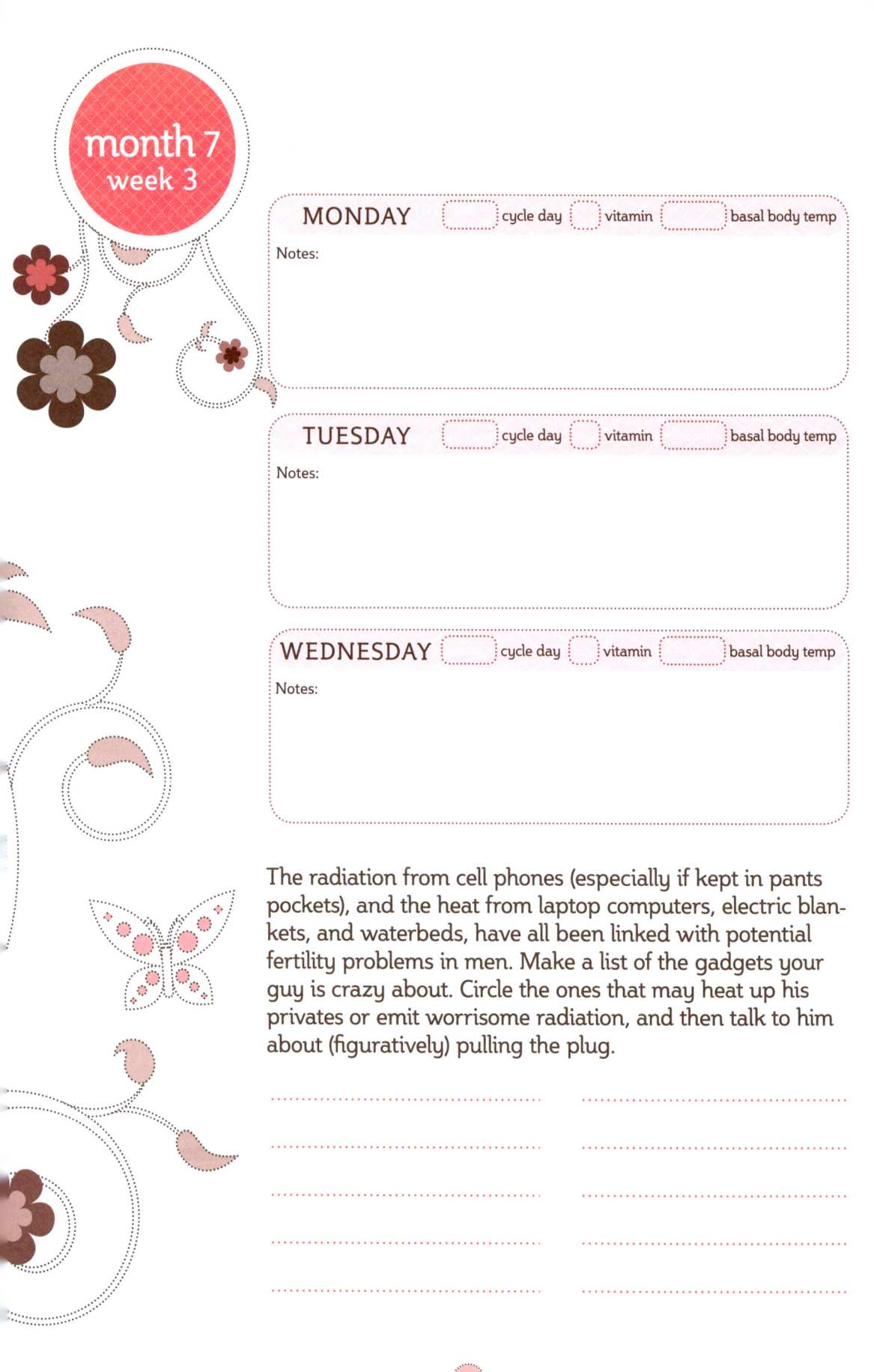

**TUESDAY** ⬚ cycle day ⬚ vitamin ⬚ basal body temp
Notes:

**WEDNESDAY** ⬚ cycle day ⬚ vitamin ⬚ basal body temp
Notes:

The radiation from cell phones (especially if kept in pants pockets), and the heat from laptop computers, electric blankets, and waterbeds, have all been linked with potential fertility problems in men. Make a list of the gadgets your guy is crazy about. Circle the ones that may heat up his privates or emit worrisome radiation, and then talk to him about (figuratively) pulling the plug.

## looking ahead to pregnancy: sympathetic pregnancy

It sounds like the stuff of television sitcoms, but some men, when their partners are pregnant, start to experience pregnancy symptoms themselves. Not to worry. It may seem weird, but your partner's nausea, indigestion, fatigue (and maybe even growing stomach) will end when you deliver. The medical term for these false pregnancy symptoms is couvade syndrome.

### THURSDAY
cycle day ___ vitamin ___ basal body temp ___
Notes:

### FRIDAY
cycle day ___ vitamin ___ basal body temp ___
Notes:

### SATURDAY
cycle day ___ vitamin ___ basal body temp ___
Notes:

### SUNDAY
cycle day ___ vitamin ___ basal body temp ___
Notes:

## can't stand the heat

Men's reproductive organs are outside the body so they can stay cooler; heat is the enemy of sperm production. For most men, wearing tight underwear instead of boxers, sitting at a desk or behind the wheel of a truck all day, or even frequenting saunas won't get in the way of conception. But if your baby-making efforts are taking longer than you'd like, it may be worth having your partner stay out of the heat for a while; it just might make the difference.

## month 7
### week 4

**MONDAY** ◯ cycle day ◯ vitamin ◯ basal body temp
Notes:

**TUESDAY** ◯ cycle day ◯ vitamin ◯ basal body temp
Notes:

**WEDNESDAY** ◯ cycle day ◯ vitamin ◯ basal body temp
Notes:

**THURSDAY** ◯ cycle day ◯ vitamin ◯ basal body temp
Notes:

## looking ahead to pregnancy: no smoking allowed

Once you're pregnant, there's no excuse for your partner to start smoking again. Exposure to secondhand smoke could jeopardize your pregnancy and cause lasting problems for your child.

## be a quitter

Cigarettes, alcohol, marijuana, and other drugs can all affect male fertility, too. Both cigarettes and marijuana affect sperm production and result in sperm abnormalities. As for alcohol, it, too, has a negative effect on sperm production, causing breakages in the DNA that can be passed to offspring. Men who are trying to get their partners pregnant should limit their alcohol consumption to no more than twice a week, with a two-drink limit each time.

### FRIDAY
cycle day | vitamin | basal body temp

Notes:

### SATURDAY
cycle day | vitamin | basal body temp

Notes:

### SUNDAY
cycle day | vitamin | basal body temp

Notes:

Write down your partner's physician's name and phone number. Now encourage him to set up an appointment. If he's had an STD, for instance, there may be scarring in his reproductive organs that would block sperm from reaching their destination. And any medications he's taking should be checked for safety, too.

NAME _____ PHONE _____

MEDICATIONS _____

# month 8

## De-stress for Success!

No, it's not as simple as "Just relax and you'll get pregnant." But stress does play a role in fertility and conception. Whether your stress is mild or severe, or comes from work deadlines or family problems, learning how to handle it can improve your general health, and up your odds of conceiving.

How would you rate your stress level now on a scale of 1 to 10?

1    2    3    4    5    6    7    8    9    10

Is your stress a daily event, or a once-in-a-while occurrence? ...............................
........................................................................................................................................
........................................................................................................................................

Do you think you deal with more or less stress
than your partner, friends, other family members? ........................................
........................................................................................................................................

We all go through stressful times. The following are generally considered to be the most stressful life events. Have you experienced any of them in the past year? (Circle all that apply.)

      Death of a loved one             Moving

      Divorce             Marriage

      Career change             Change in health status

How do you handle the stress in your life? ...........................................................
........................................................................................................................................
........................................................................................................................................

# month 8 week 1

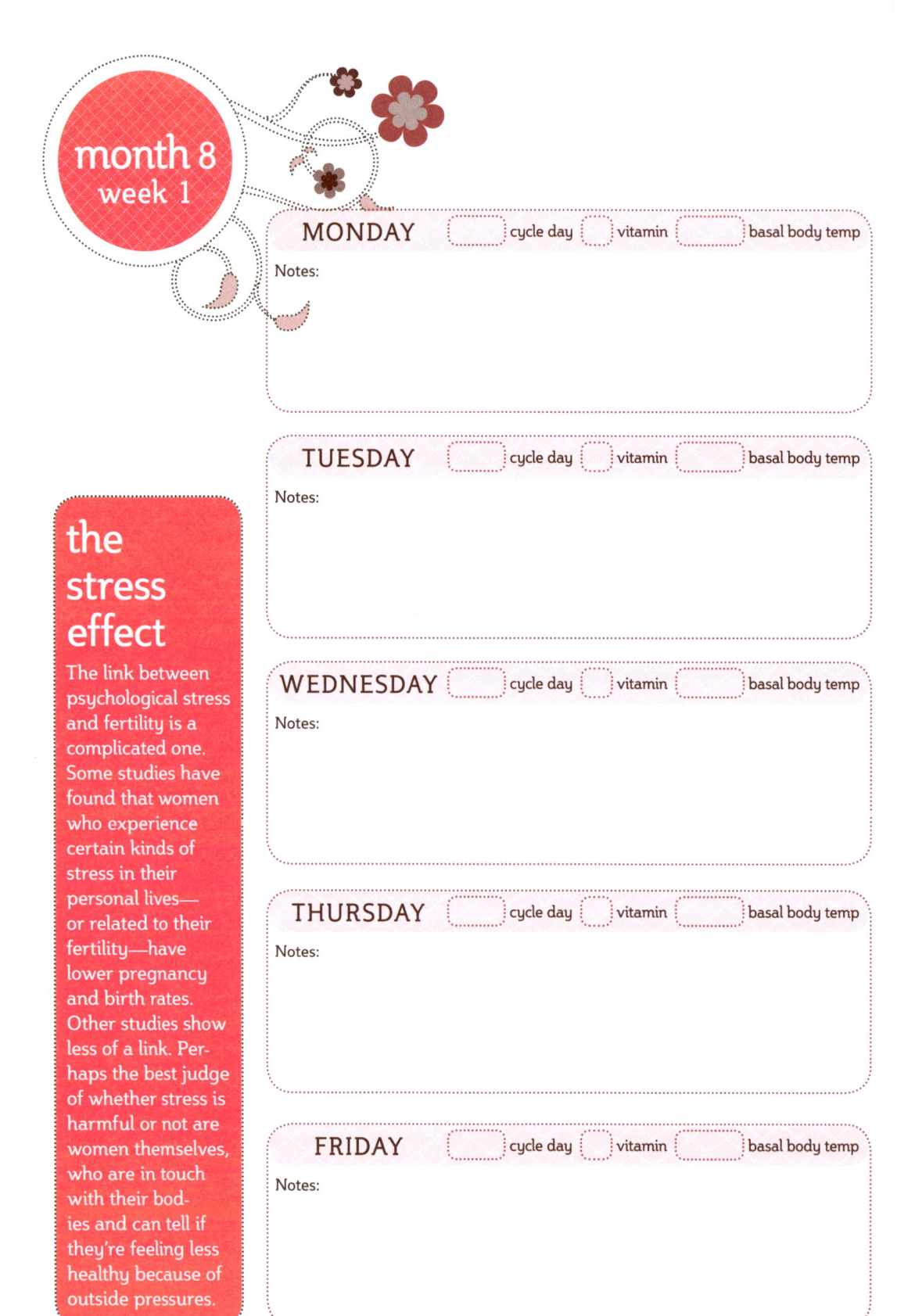

**MONDAY** — cycle day — vitamin — basal body temp

Notes:

**TUESDAY** — cycle day — vitamin — basal body temp

Notes:

**WEDNESDAY** — cycle day — vitamin — basal body temp

Notes:

**THURSDAY** — cycle day — vitamin — basal body temp

Notes:

**FRIDAY** — cycle day — vitamin — basal body temp

Notes:

## the stress effect

The link between psychological stress and fertility is a complicated one. Some studies have found that women who experience certain kinds of stress in their personal lives—or related to their fertility—have lower pregnancy and birth rates. Other studies show less of a link. Perhaps the best judge of whether stress is harmful or not are women themselves, who are in touch with their bodies and can tell if they're feeling less healthy because of outside pressures.

# looking ahead to pregnancy: worry

Worrying keeps many women from fully enjoying their pregnancies. Try to keep your worries in check by taking good care of yourself and going for regular prenatal check-ups. Then relax, knowing you've done everything possible to ensure a healthy baby.

**SATURDAY**    cycle day    vitamin    basal body temp

Notes:

**SUNDAY**    cycle day    vitamin    basal body temp

Notes:

What can you change to eliminate stress from your life?

.......................................................................................................................................

.......................................................................................................................................

What can't be changed . . . but must be dealt with?

.......................................................................................................................................

.......................................................................................................................................

Don't forget that some stress is actually a positive, motivating force. Is your stress the good kind, the bad kind . . . or both?

.......................................................................................................................................

.......................................................................................................................................

## month 8
### week 2

**MONDAY** — cycle day — vitamin — basal body temp
Notes:

**TUESDAY** — cycle day — vitamin — basal body temp
Notes:

**WEDNESDAY** — cycle day — vitamin — basal body temp
Notes:

Stress relief doesn't require any kind of formal meditation or yoga program unless you want it to. Exercise, crafts, even coffee dates with girlfriends can all help you handle daily pressure. Make a list of the activities that you find most relaxing.

**THURSDAY** ⬚ cycle day ⬚ vitamin ⬚ basal body temp
Notes:

**FRIDAY** ⬚ cycle day ⬚ vitamin ⬚ basal body temp
Notes:

**SATURDAY** ⬚ cycle day ⬚ vitamin ⬚ basal body temp
Notes:

**SUNDAY** ⬚ cycle day ⬚ vitamin ⬚ basal body temp
Notes:

## the science of stress

Ovulation is triggered when the hypothalamus gland, located near the base of the brain, secretes gonadotropin-releasing hormone (GnRH), which signals the pituitary gland to release luteinizing hormone (LH) and follicle-stimulating hormone (FSH). But during times of stress, the hypothalamus may start releasing corticotropin-releasing hormone (CRH), which can reduce or block the GnRH signal. Periods may become irregular or absent, and ovulation may not occur.

## looking ahead to pregnancy: more stress science

The same stress hormones that can block ovulation can also interfere with normal pregnancy development. Studies have shown that pregnant women who experience severe stress are at risk of preterm labor and low birthweight babies.

# month 8
## week 3

**MONDAY**  ◯ cycle day  ◯ vitamin  ◯ basal body temp
Notes:

**TUESDAY**  ◯ cycle day  ◯ vitamin  ◯ basal body temp
Notes:

**WEDNESDAY**  ◯ cycle day  ◯ vitamin  ◯ basal body temp
Notes:

## chicken or egg
Some researchers wonder if part of the unhealthy effect of stress has as much to do with how it affects lifestyle as hormones. In other words, women under stress probably don't eat as healthily, sleep as well, or work out as regularly as women who are feeling more relaxed and in control of their lives. To minimize the effect of stress on your health and fertility, make sure to continue your healthy good habits even when stress makes you want to reach for a chocolate bar (or martini!).

**THURSDAY**  ◯ cycle day  ◯ vitamin  ◯ basal body temp
Notes:

# looking ahead to pregnancy: sleep it off

Sleep is one of the best ways to regenerate and deal with stress when you're pregnant. Aim for a relatively early bedtime and try a glass of warm milk before bed. This old home remedy is especially useful during pregnancy since it also adds more calcium to your diet.

**FRIDAY**   cycle day   vitamin   basal body temp

Notes:

**SATURDAY**   cycle day   vitamin   basal body temp

Notes:

**SUNDAY**   cycle day   vitamin   basal body temp

Notes:

Imaging—using the power of your mind to conjure up relaxing thoughts—is one way some people deal with stress. Describe the most relaxing scene you can think of—swaying palm trees? Beautiful sunset? Fields of wildflowers? Then conjure it up whenever you need a calming thought.

# month 8
## week 4

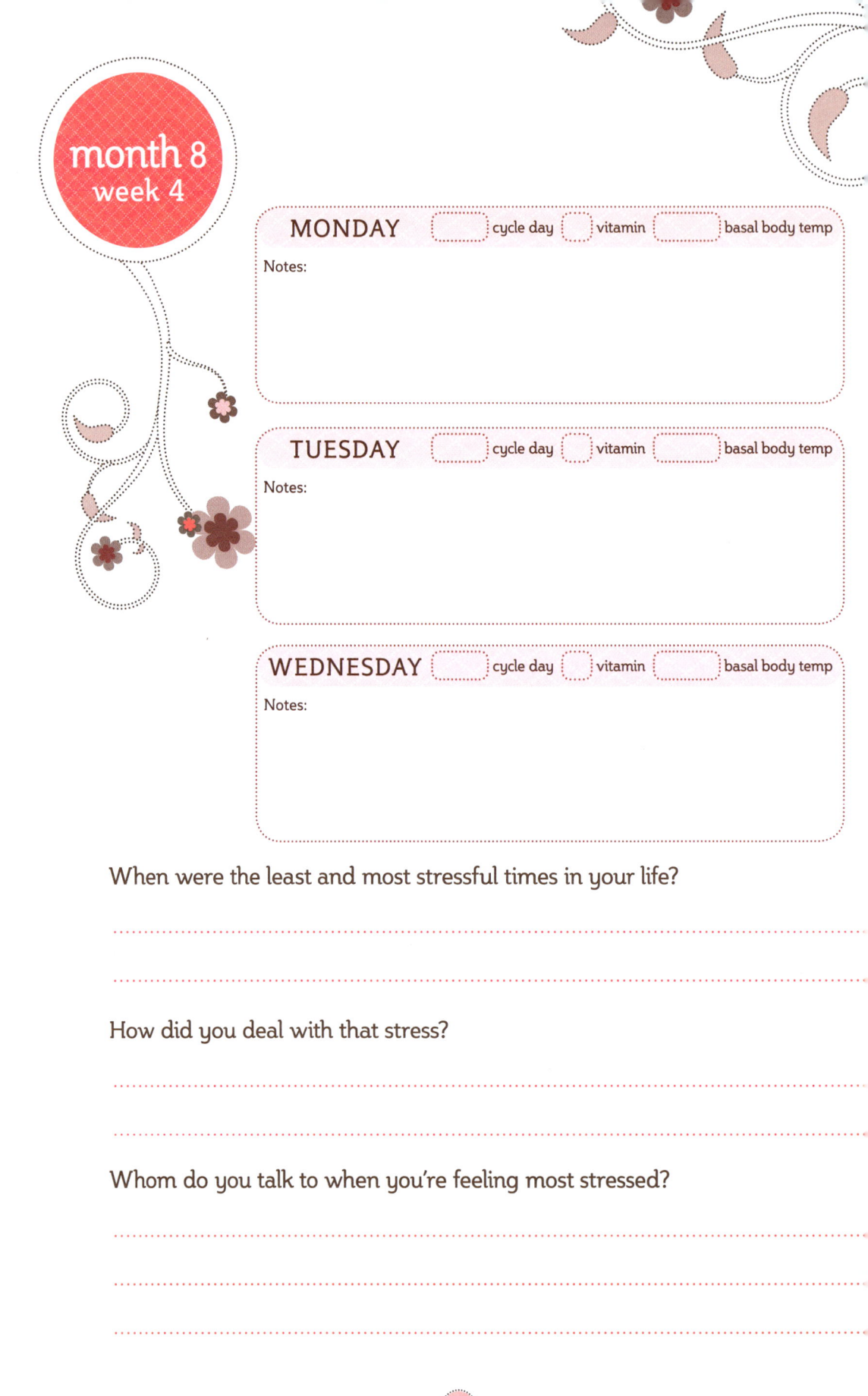

**MONDAY** ( ) cycle day ( ) vitamin ( ) basal body temp
Notes:

**TUESDAY** ( ) cycle day ( ) vitamin ( ) basal body temp
Notes:

**WEDNESDAY** ( ) cycle day ( ) vitamin ( ) basal body temp
Notes:

When were the least and most stressful times in your life?

How did you deal with that stress?

Whom do you talk to when you're feeling most stressed?

# looking ahead to pregnancy: talk it out

Before stress has a chance of jeopardizing your pregnancy, find someone to talk to about what's going on in your life. Talk to your baby's father, your best girlfriend, your mother, or anyone else you can confide in. You can also join a pregnancy support group to commiserate with other women who are experiencing the same things. If you need to, make an appointment with a counselor or therapist for some professional one-on-one help.

### THURSDAY   cycle day   vitamin   basal body temp
Notes:

### FRIDAY   cycle day   vitamin   basal body temp
Notes:

### SATURDAY   cycle day   vitamin   basal body temp
Notes:

### SUNDAY   cycle day   vitamin   basal body temp
Notes:

## to each her own . . . stress

Reactions to stress, and health effects from it, are incredibly individual. Some women may remain cheerful and calm in the face of total chaos, while others are fazed by even small challenges. That means stress may be a factor in conception for some women, but not for others. But if you're in the stressed-out camp, don't blame yourself. Other things that are more under your control—like nutrition and lifestyle—are an even more important factor in fertility.

# month 9

## Get Up and Move It

Now isn't the time to sit down and wait for conception to happen. Exercising will help you get in good shape for pregnancy, and also get you into a regular fitness rhythm that you can continue—perhaps with some modifications—right up until delivery. The most important thing of all is just to do it . . . for a healthy conception, pregnancy, and beyond.

Do you exercise regularly?   ◯ Yes   ◯ No

What do you like best about exercise? ..................................................................
..........................................................................................................................
..........................................................................................................................

What do you dislike? ........................................................................................
..........................................................................................................................
..........................................................................................................................

What kinds of activities did you think were fun when you were a kid? ................
..........................................................................................................................
..........................................................................................................................
..........................................................................................................................

What exercises or sports do you enjoy watching on television? ........................
..........................................................................................................................
..........................................................................................................................
..........................................................................................................................

What activities or sports would you try if time—or money—were no object? ........
..........................................................................................................................
..........................................................................................................................
..........................................................................................................................

# month 9
## week 1

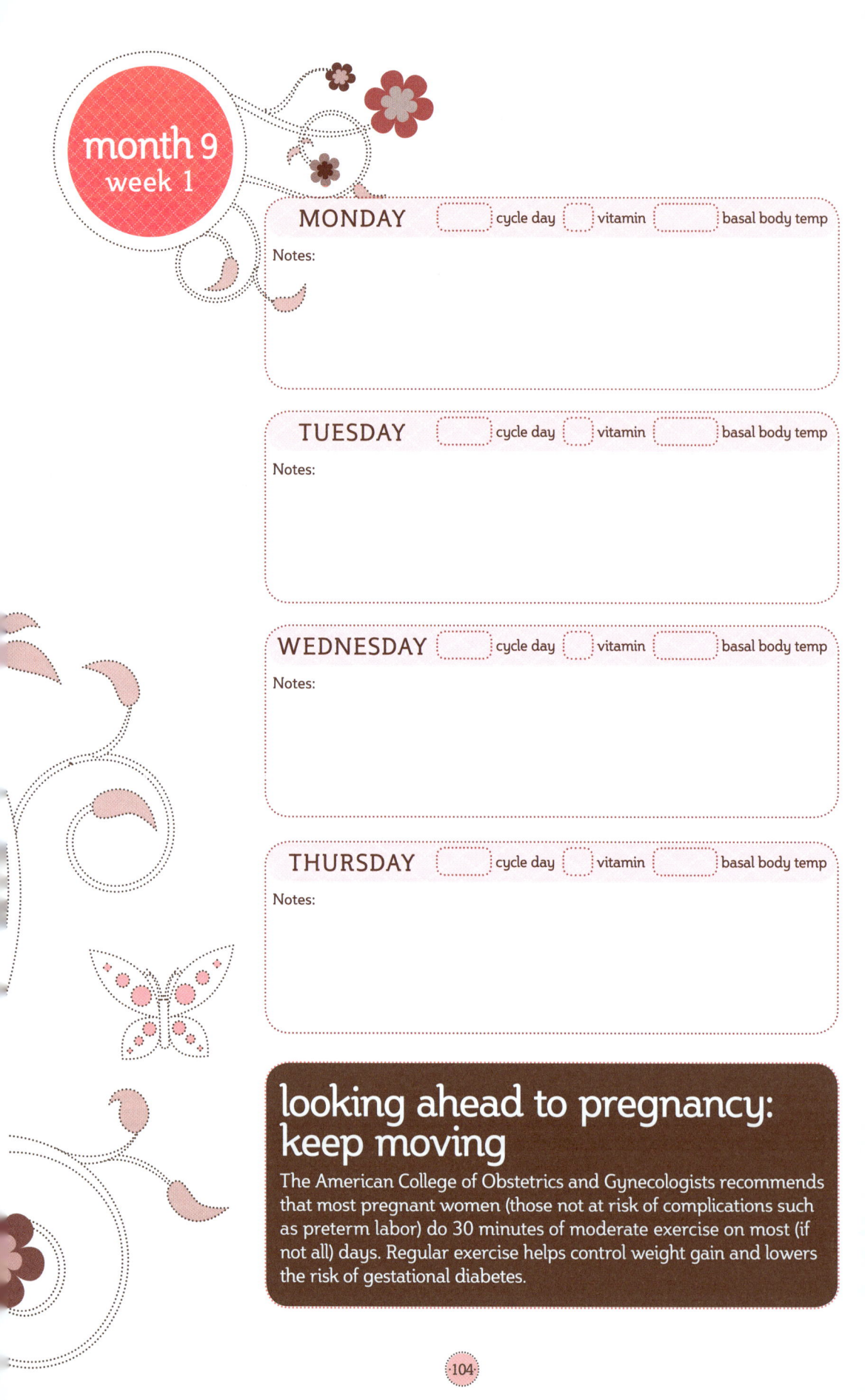

**MONDAY**  ⬚ cycle day  ⬚ vitamin  ⬚ basal body temp

Notes:

**TUESDAY**  ⬚ cycle day  ⬚ vitamin  ⬚ basal body temp

Notes:

**WEDNESDAY**  ⬚ cycle day  ⬚ vitamin  ⬚ basal body temp

Notes:

**THURSDAY**  ⬚ cycle day  ⬚ vitamin  ⬚ basal body temp

Notes:

## looking ahead to pregnancy: keep moving

The American College of Obstetrics and Gynecologists recommends that most pregnant women (those not at risk of complications such as preterm labor) do 30 minutes of moderate exercise on most (if not all) days. Regular exercise helps control weight gain and lowers the risk of gestational diabetes.

## start now

If you're a regular exerciser, keep it up. If not, don't think you can use trying to conceive as an excuse to stay on the couch. Regular exercise can benefit general health, and sometimes even increase fertility. And since you're not pregnant yet, there are no restrictions to what you can do for fitness. If you love in-line skates, start rolling. Ever wished you could be on a woman's volleyball or soccer team? Join up.

### FRIDAY  cycle day ___  vitamin ___  basal body temp ___
Notes:

### SATURDAY  cycle day ___  vitamin ___  basal body temp ___
Notes:

### SUNDAY  cycle day ___  vitamin ___  basal body temp ___
Notes:

Are any or all of your friends into working out? Maybe there's one who does Pilates, another who walks, and still another who uses the weight machines at the gym. List your friends and their fitness habits here, then see if there's someone you can join for regular exercise.

..................................  ..................................  ..................................

..................................  ..................................  ..................................

..................................  ..................................  ..................................

# month 9 week 2

**MONDAY** ⬚ cycle day ⬚ vitamin ⬚ basal body temp
Notes:

**TUESDAY** ⬚ cycle day ⬚ vitamin ⬚ basal body temp
Notes:

**WEDNESDAY** ⬚ cycle day ⬚ vitamin ⬚ basal body temp
Notes:

**THURSDAY** ⬚ cycle day ⬚ vitamin ⬚ basal body temp
Notes:

## the best exercise for fertility...

is the one you like enough to do regularly. More important than what you do is how often you do it. Getting on the treadmill three times a week is better than going outside to run just once. And here's a case where money doesn't matter. You don't need to join a gym or hire a personal trainer to get in shape. Take a brisk walk outside, put on the radio and start dancing, or climb the ten flights of stairs to your office every day.

## looking ahead to pregnancy: what to modify

While most exercises are considered fine during pregnancy, there are exceptions. Pregnant women should limit exercises that involve long periods of lying down, as well as anything that might cause dizziness, falls, or abdominal injury (examples: soccer, skiing, horseback riding, bicycling, gymnastics). Scuba diving should also be avoided.

Are you a rock 'n roll girl? Into rap or hip-hop? Prefer old show tunes? Whatever you're into, use it to motivate you while you're working out. Bring some of your favorite songs to work out to. Start with some slow numbers for a warm-up, increase the tempo and keep it nice and fast for at least 20 minutes, then end with some peaceful, relaxing music. Write your ideal fitness playlist here:

**FRIDAY** — cycle day — vitamin — basal body temp
Notes:

**SATURDAY** — cycle day — vitamin — basal body temp
Notes:

**SUNDAY** — cycle day — vitamin — basal body temp
Notes:

# month 9
## week 3

**MONDAY** ( ) cycle day ( ) vitamin ( ) basal body temp

Notes:

**TUESDAY** ( ) cycle day ( ) vitamin ( ) basal body temp

Notes:

## can you exercise too much to conceive?

Conventional wisdom held that exercising too much could cause women to stop ovulating. But now studies have shown that it's not too much exercise that's the problem, but too little nutrition to support it. When you want to become pregnant, you can exercise as much as you'd like, provided you consume enough calories to keep your body mass index above 18. Think of those extra calories as another one of exercise's benefits!

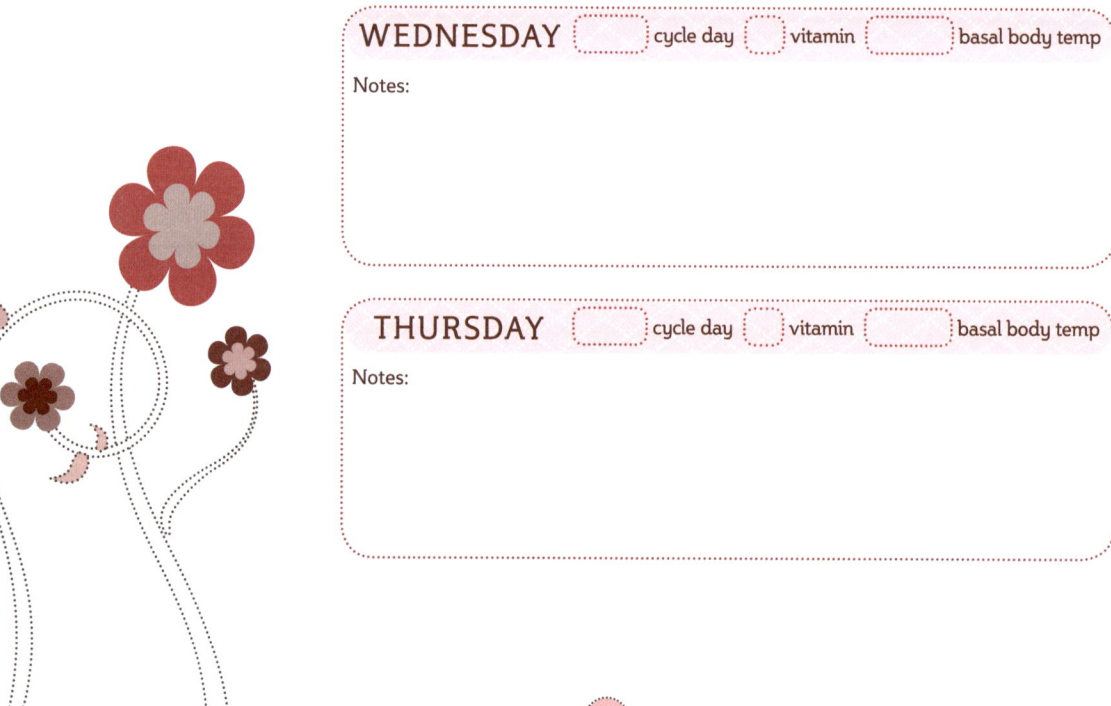

**WEDNESDAY** ( ) cycle day ( ) vitamin ( ) basal body temp

Notes:

**THURSDAY** ( ) cycle day ( ) vitamin ( ) basal body temp

Notes:

Start clipping pictures from magazines of cute fitness clothes that will make you want to get up and move. Go for skintight or midriff-baring if you dare, but there are plenty more options. Cute sneakers, comfy yoga pants, a funny T-shirt, and a good sports bra are really all you need for most workouts. Write your fitness shopping list here:

..................................................................................................................................

..................................................................................................................................

..................................................................................................................................

### FRIDAY    cycle day    vitamin    basal body temp
Notes:

### SATURDAY    cycle day    vitamin    basal body temp
Notes:

### SUNDAY    cycle day    vitamin    basal body temp
Notes:

# looking ahead to pregnancy: maternity fitness fashion

Exercising during pregnancy no longer means huge shapeless T-shirts over elastic-waist pants. A whole range of adorable workout clothes—from bike shorts to bikinis—is now available for pregnant women, too.

## month 9 week 4

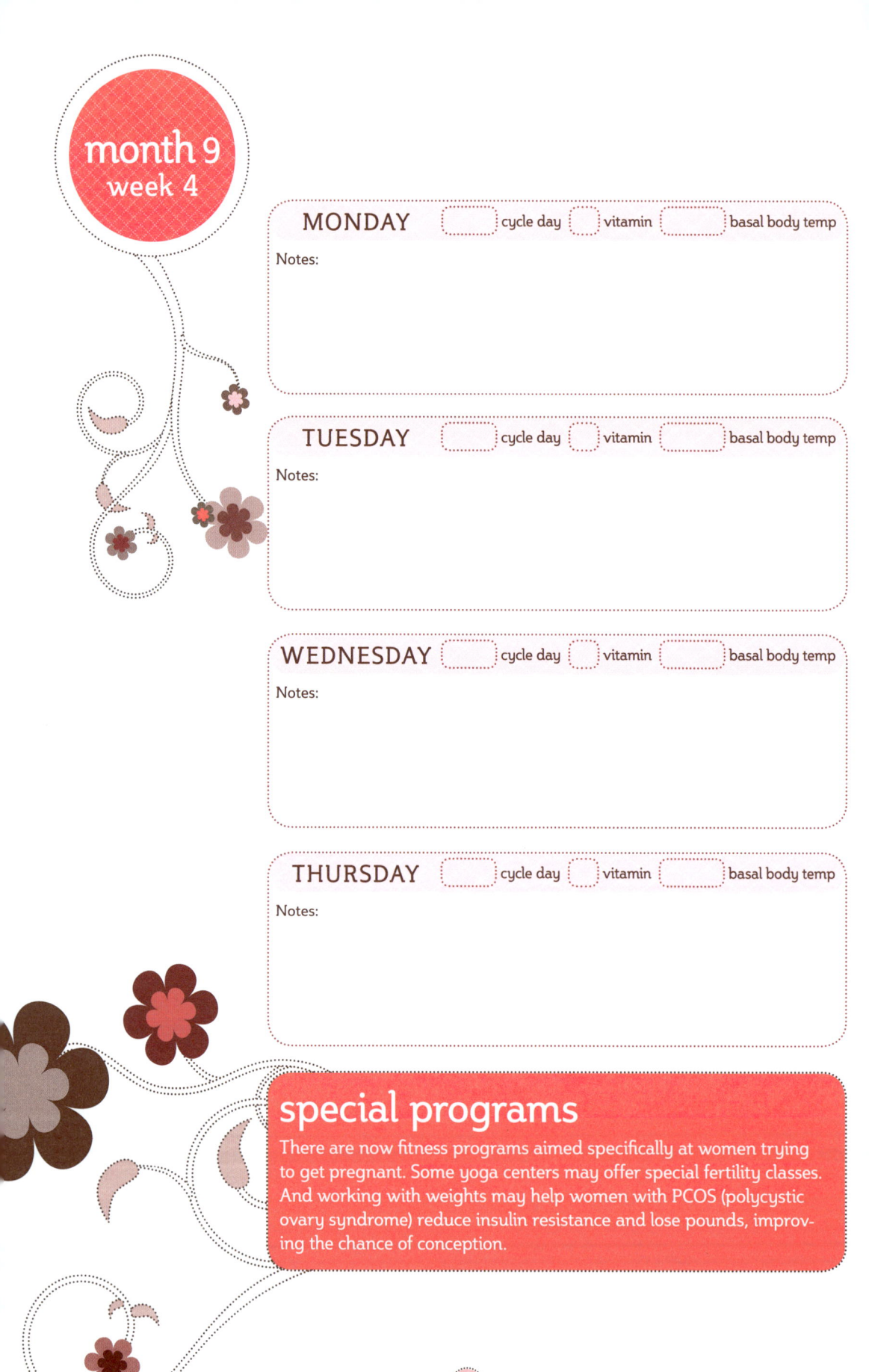

**MONDAY** ☐ cycle day ☐ vitamin ☐ basal body temp

Notes:

**TUESDAY** ☐ cycle day ☐ vitamin ☐ basal body temp

Notes:

**WEDNESDAY** ☐ cycle day ☐ vitamin ☐ basal body temp

Notes:

**THURSDAY** ☐ cycle day ☐ vitamin ☐ basal body temp

Notes:

## special programs

There are now fitness programs aimed specifically at women trying to get pregnant. Some yoga centers may offer special fertility classes. And working with weights may help women with PCOS (polycystic ovary syndrome) reduce insulin resistance and lose pounds, improving the chance of conception.

## looking ahead to pregnancy: videos just for you

If maintaining a gym membership during pregnancy seems too expensive, or you're too embarrassed to show up with a big beautiful pregnancy belly (we say flaunt it!), you can still get great workouts at home with any of dozens of pregnancy workout videos.

**FRIDAY** ☐ cycle day ☐ vitamin ☐ basal body temp
Notes:

**SATURDAY** ☐ cycle day ☐ vitamin ☐ basal body temp
Notes:

**SUNDAY** ☐ cycle day ☐ vitamin ☐ basal body temp
Notes:

Many women say they're too busy to exercise, but women who exercise regularly say the increased energy they get from working out more than makes up for the time they spend on fitness. If you think you're too busy to exercise, try setting aside just five minutes, three or four times this week. Next week increase it to 10, then 20, etc. Before three months are over your workouts will be up to an hour long.

# month 10

## Pamper Yourself

Soon you'll be taking care of a new baby, but for now your prime concern is you. Find the time to indulge yourself as much as possible. Whether it's luxury spa weekends or just wonderful backrubs from your partner, make pampering a part of your life. You may feel busy now, but trust us—you'll be even busier once you're a mom!

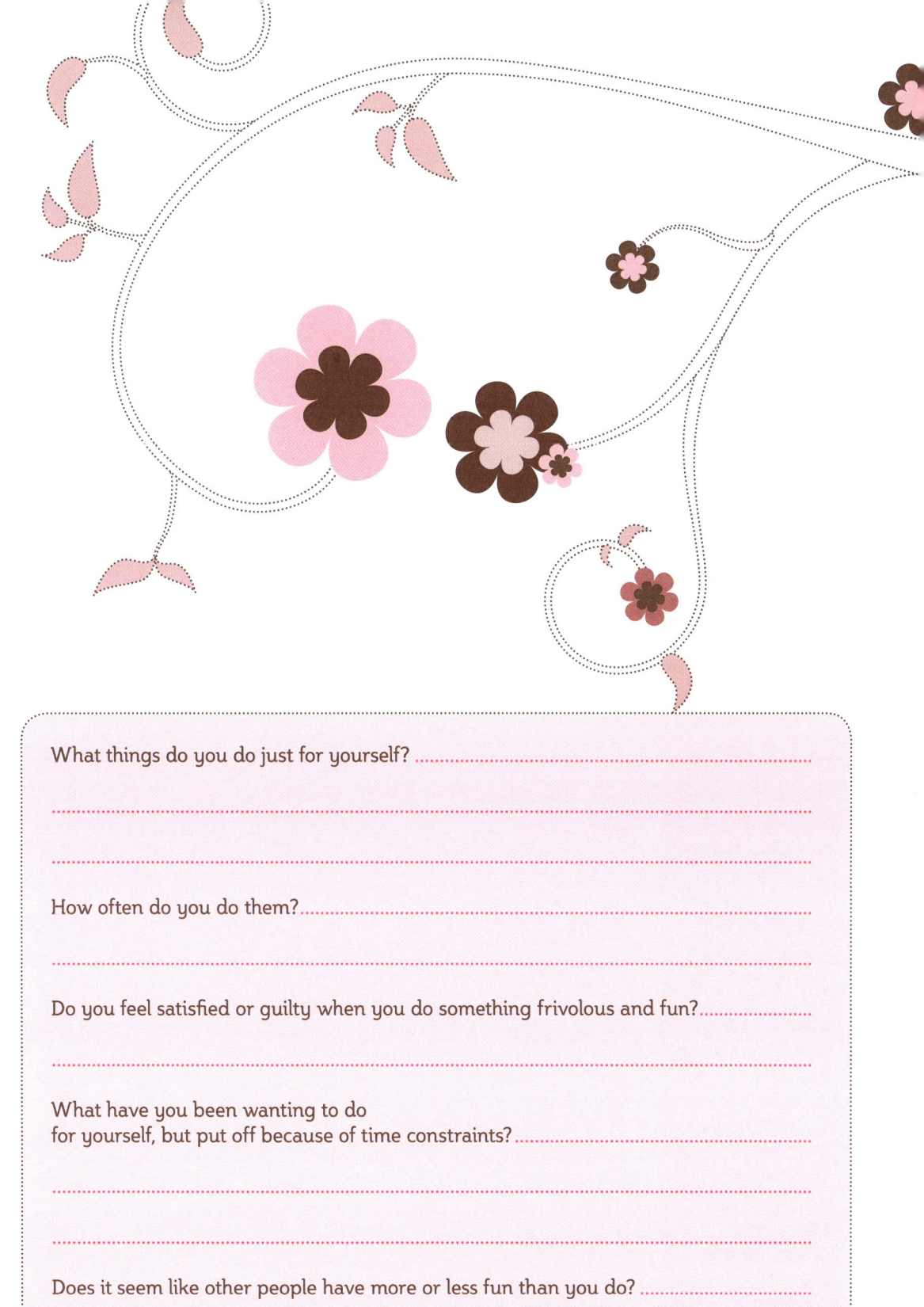

What things do you do just for yourself?

How often do you do them?

Do you feel satisfied or guilty when you do something frivolous and fun?

What have you been wanting to do for yourself, but put off because of time constraints?

Does it seem like other people have more or less fun than you do?

# month 10 week 1

**MONDAY** ☐ cycle day ☐ vitamin ☐ basal body temp
Notes:

**TUESDAY** ☐ cycle day ☐ vitamin ☐ basal body temp
Notes:

**WEDNESDAY** ☐ cycle day ☐ vitamin ☐ basal body temp
Notes:

**THURSDAY** ☐ cycle day ☐ vitamin ☐ basal body temp
Notes:

**FRIDAY** ☐ cycle day ☐ vitamin ☐ basal body temp
Notes:

## get over the guilt

It's not selfish, it's smart to pamper yourself. Treating yourself to pleasurable things means you care about yourself and keeping yourself happy. Remember what they say on an airplane when they instruct the passengers on the use of oxygen masks—you have to put the mask on yourself before you assist others. In the same way, you need to learn how to take good care of yourself now, so you can take good care of your family soon.

# looking ahead to pregnancy: prenatal pampering

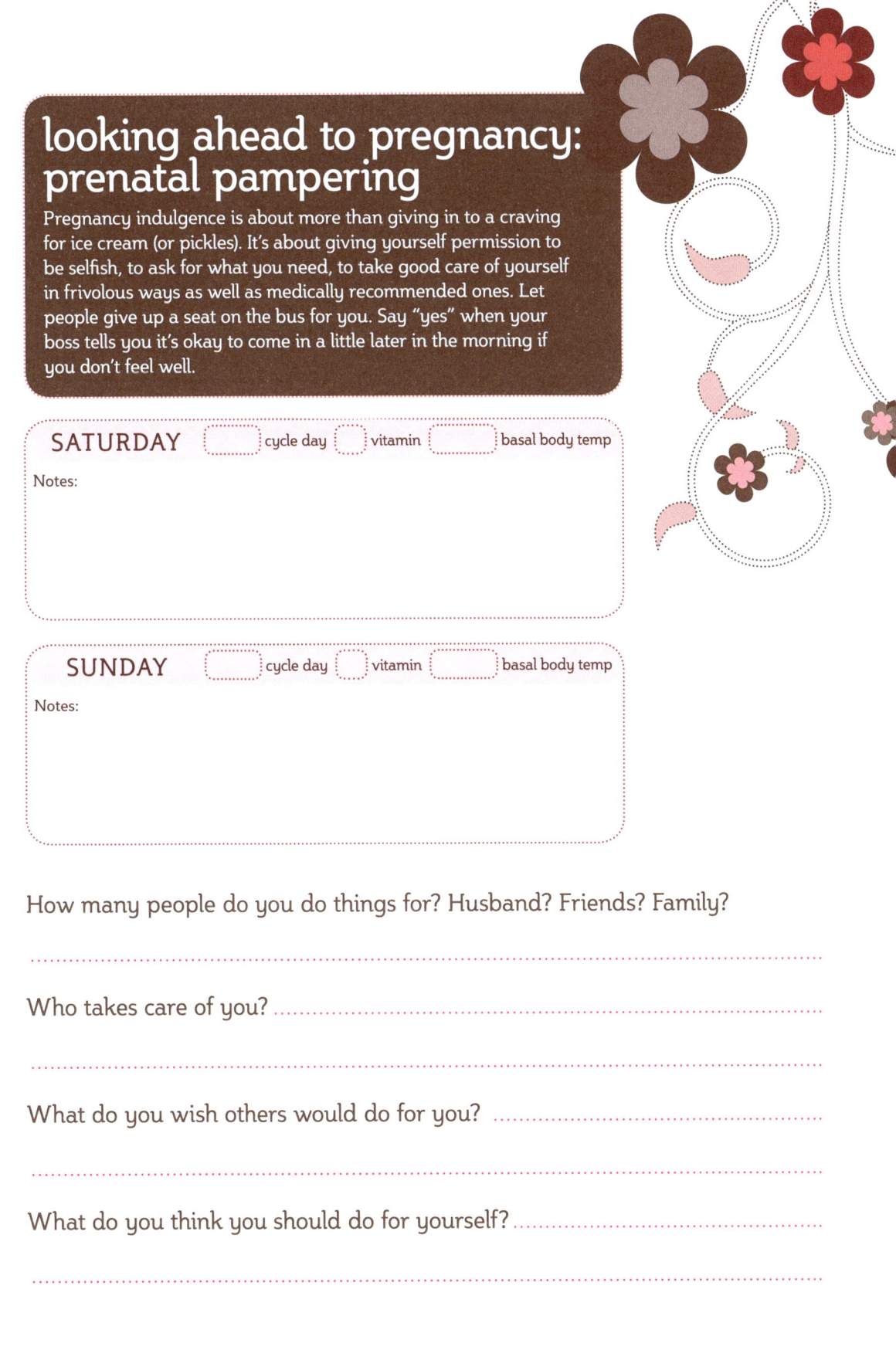

Pregnancy indulgence is about more than giving in to a craving for ice cream (or pickles). It's about giving yourself permission to be selfish, to ask for what you need, to take good care of yourself in frivolous ways as well as medically recommended ones. Let people give up a seat on the bus for you. Say "yes" when your boss tells you it's okay to come in a little later in the morning if you don't feel well.

**SATURDAY**  ☐ cycle day  ☐ vitamin  ☐ basal body temp

Notes:

**SUNDAY**  ☐ cycle day  ☐ vitamin  ☐ basal body temp

Notes:

How many people do you do things for? Husband? Friends? Family?

................................................................................................................

Who takes care of you? ......................................................................

................................................................................................................

What do you wish others would do for you? ...................................

................................................................................................................

What do you think you should do for yourself? ...............................

................................................................................................................

## month 10
### week 2

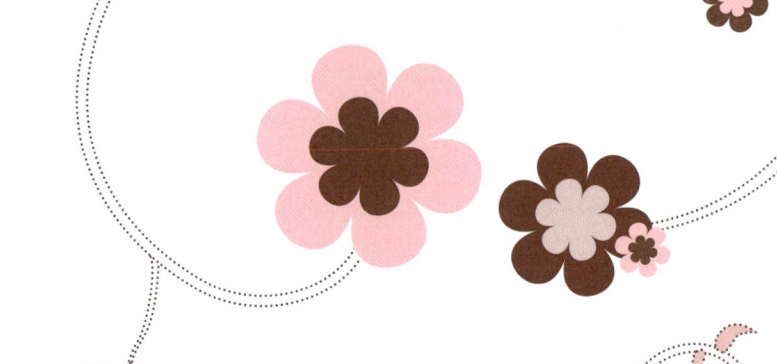

## prepregnancy indulgences

Now is a great time to think about the things you want for yourself—besides a baby, of course. Being a parent sometimes means putting your own needs second, but right now you can still treat yourself as number one. Schedule some beauty and body maintenance treatments, and let yourself go on a shopping spree once in a while. You deserve it.

**MONDAY** — cycle day — vitamin — basal body temp

Notes:

**TUESDAY** — cycle day — vitamin — basal body temp

Notes:

## looking ahead to pregnancy: you can still indulge!

You certainly don't have to give up your beauty routine because you're pregnant. Not only will your skin have that wonderful pregnancy glow, but your hair may become thicker and shinier than normal. Beauty treatments like facials, gentle massages, manicures and pedicures (but avoid excessive exposure to fumes), and waxing (on any part of the body) are generally fine, but if you're worried check with your doctor to be sure.

| WEDNESDAY | cycle day | vitamin | basal body temp |

Notes:

| THURSDAY | cycle day | vitamin | basal body temp |

Notes:

| FRIDAY | cycle day | vitamin | basal body temp |

Notes:

| SATURDAY | cycle day | vitamin | basal body temp |

Notes:

| SUNDAY | cycle day | vitamin | basal body temp |

Notes:

When is the last time you had a massage?

..................................

A facial?

..................................

Met a girlfriend for a mani/pedi?

..................................

Wandered around a museum?

..................................

Scored a ticket to a hot concert?

..................................

If your answers surprise you, then you're overdue for some serious fun. What would you like to do for yourself now?

..................................
..................................
..................................

# month 10
## week 3

**MONDAY**  ⬚ cycle day  ⬚ vitamin  ⬚ basal body temp

Notes:

**TUESDAY**  ⬚ cycle day  ⬚ vitamin  ⬚ basal body temp

Notes:

**WEDNESDAY**  ⬚ cycle day  ⬚ vitamin  ⬚ basal body temp

Notes:

## pampering doesn't have to mean pricey

If you're thinking that spa services, shopping sprees, and other indulgences sound like fun but also sound expensive, there are plenty of other ways to treat yourself without spending a lot. Instead of visiting a spa, organize a girls' spa night at your house, where you and your friends give each other facials and manicures. Instead of expensive jewelry, bring home trendy costume pieces and other fun accessories you can wear straight through pregnancy.

What are your favorite expensive indulgences?

What inexpensive treats can take their place?

# looking ahead to pregnancy: proceed with caution

While most beauty treatments are fine to continue during pregnancy, there are a few things that should be avoided. Anything involving heat (saunas, steam rooms, hot rocks, body wraps) is a bad idea, as are many things involving chemicals (teeth bleaching, Botox, and excessive exposure to fumes from nail polish and polish removers). Hair coloring is usually okay after the first trimester. Check with your doctor before using any chemical products or undergoing any invasive procedures.

### THURSDAY     cycle day     vitamin     basal body temp
Notes:

### FRIDAY     cycle day     vitamin     basal body temp
Notes:

### SATURDAY     cycle day     vitamin     basal body temp
Notes:

### SUNDAY     cycle day     vitamin     basal body temp
Notes:

# month 10
## week 4

**MONDAY** ⬚ cycle day ⬚ vitamin ⬚ basal body temp
Notes:

**TUESDAY** ⬚ cycle day ⬚ vitamin ⬚ basal body temp
Notes:

**WEDNESDAY** ⬚ cycle day ⬚ vitamin ⬚ basal body temp
Notes:

**THURSDAY** ⬚ cycle day ⬚ vitamin ⬚ basal body temp
Notes:

## gal-palling around

Your efforts to get pregnant mainly involve you and your partner, of course, but that doesn't mean other people shouldn't be important in your life, too. Girlfriends are an especially valuable source of emotional support, fertility and pregnancy information, and just good company. You're going to need them more than ever now, soon, and later.

## looking ahead to pregnancy: the mom-to-be club

Even if you have a large group of great friends, you might still enjoy sharing your pregnancy experience with other women who are going through it at the same time. Look online for support groups, and talk to the women in your obstetrician's waiting room, or at your childbirth education classes. Pregnancy is a powerful time for female bonding.

Who are your best girlfriends?
..................................................................................................................................

How many of them are moms? ................................................................................................
..................................................................................................................................

Do you ever talk about your dreams of parenthood together? ........................
..................................................................................................................................

What's the best advice you ever got from a friend? ...........................................
..................................................................................................................................

The best advice you've ever given? ........................................................................
..................................................................................................................................

**FRIDAY**  ⬚ cycle day  ⬚ vitamin  ⬚ basal body temp

Notes:



**SATURDAY**  ⬚ cycle day  ⬚ vitamin  ⬚ basal body temp

Notes:



**SUNDAY**  ⬚ cycle day  ⬚ vitamin  ⬚ basal body temp

Notes:

# month 11

## Relationship Rx

On the journey to conception, pregnancy, and parenthood, sometimes a couple's relationship can get sidetracked. Focused on the goal of getting pregnant, you may temporarily forget that other parts of your life together are important, too. Your relationship is the foundation on which your future family will be built, and it's important that you keep that foundation strong and happy.

What first attracted you to your partner? ...................................................................................
................................................................................................................................................
................................................................................................................................................

What are his best physical attributes? ......................................................................................
................................................................................................................................................

What are his best personality traits? ........................................................................................
................................................................................................................................................
................................................................................................................................................

When is the last time the two of you went out on a date? ....................................................
................................................................................................................................................
................................................................................................................................................

What do you like to talk about together? ................................................................................
................................................................................................................................................
................................................................................................................................................

What hobbies and interests do you share? ..............................................................................
................................................................................................................................................
................................................................................................................................................
................................................................................................................................................

When did you last have sex just for fun, and not to reproduce? ............................................
................................................................................................................................................
................................................................................................................................................

# month 11
## week 1

**MONDAY** | cycle day | vitamin | basal body temp

Notes:

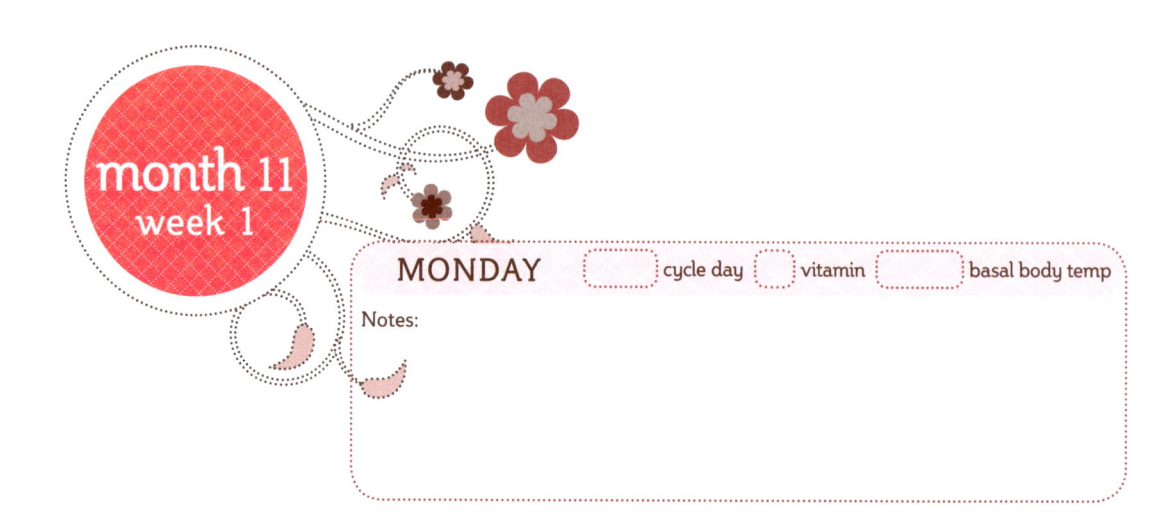

## communication: men are from mars . . .

Keep the lines of communication open. You can't assume that your partner is thinking or feeling the same things you are. For instance, you might be thinking about your cycle each month as a new chance for pregnancy, while your husband is thinking about ovulation as his sure bet for frequent sex.

**TUESDAY** | cycle day | vitamin | basal body temp

Notes:

**WEDNESDAY** | cycle day | vitamin | basal body temp

Notes:

**THURSDAY** | cycle day | vitamin | basal body temp

Notes:

Scheduling some time every few days, or once a week, to talk about your procreation efforts may help keep both of you sane. Use the time to make sure you're both on the same page, and in sync about your timetable and about what comes next. Jot down some talking points here.

..............................................................................................

..............................................................................................

..............................................................................................

..............................................................................................

**FRIDAY**  ☐ cycle day  ☐ vitamin  ☐ basal body temp

Notes:

**SATURDAY**  ☐ cycle day  ☐ vitamin  ☐ basal body temp

Notes:

# looking ahead to pregnancy: keep talking . . .

The dialogue with your partner started when you were dating, has continued through your marriage, and got you through trying to conceive. Now you're pregnant, and the conversation should still be going strong. You'll have even more to talk about soon.

**SUNDAY**  ☐ cycle day  ☐ vitamin  ☐ basal body temp

Notes:

# month 11
## week 2

**MONDAY** — cycle day — vitamin — basal body temp
Notes:

**TUESDAY** — cycle day — vitamin — basal body temp
Notes:

**WEDNESDAY** — cycle day — vitamin — basal body temp
Notes:

What's the most romantic thing your partner ever did for you? ..............................
......................................................................................................................

What romantic things have you done for him? ..............................................
......................................................................................................................

How long ago was your last romantic experience together? ..............................
......................................................................................................................

What can you do now to bring romance back into your lives? ............................
......................................................................................................................

## looking ahead to pregnancy: keep it steamy

Morning sickness and fatigue might make feeling romantic and sexy more of a challenge, and that goes for nighttime infant feedings, too. But if you need any more proof that motherhood can be sexy, check out the latest maternity negligees, lacy bras, and even wispy thongs. If sexy is a state of mind, then it's perfectly compatible with parenthood.

**THURSDAY** ( ) cycle day ( ) vitamin ( ) basal body temp
Notes:

**FRIDAY** ( ) cycle day ( ) vitamin ( ) basal body temp
Notes:

**SATURDAY** ( ) cycle day ( ) vitamin ( ) basal body temp
Notes:

**SUNDAY** ( ) cycle day ( ) vitamin ( ) basal body temp
Notes:

### real-life romance

Keeping connected romantically when you're trying to conceive doesn't have to be complicated. Daily gestures like gazing into each other's eyes, dancing around the kitchen to a great song, leaving sweet notes in each other's briefcases, or touching at unexpected moments can all keep the mood loving, even when schedules are tight.

# month 11 week 3

**MONDAY**  ( ) cycle day  ( ) vitamin  ( ) basal body temp
Notes:

**TUESDAY**  ( ) cycle day  ( ) vitamin  ( ) basal body temp
Notes:

**WEDNESDAY**  ( ) cycle day  ( ) vitamin  ( ) basal body temp
Notes:

**THURSDAY**  ( ) cycle day  ( ) vitamin  ( ) basal body temp
Notes:

**FRIDAY**  ( ) cycle day  ( ) vitamin  ( ) basal body temp
Notes:

## keep your sense of humor and have fun together

Fertility can seem like a serious subject, but it's important to keep your sense of humor. Peeing on a stick to see if you're pregnant is pretty funny when you think about it. So is having to make love when a fertility monitor tells you to. Keep laughing.

# looking ahead to pregnancy: the fun continues

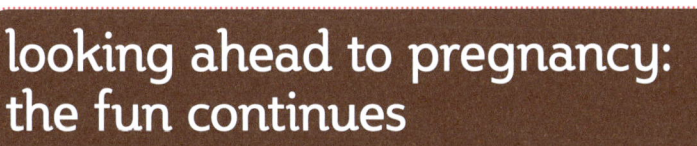

Don't lose your sense of humor now. If you can laugh at morning sickness—and having to run out of a company meeting to throw up—then you'll be able to laugh later when you see your best business outfit has a spit-up stain on the left shoulder. A sense of humor is vital to parenthood!

**SATURDAY**  ⬚ cycle day  ⬚ vitamin  ⬚ basal body temp

Notes:

**SUNDAY**  ⬚ cycle day  ⬚ vitamin  ⬚ basal body temp

Notes:

Who has the better sense of humor, you or your partner? ................................

How does your partner make you laugh? How do you make him laugh? ................

What's the funniest story you can tell about trying to conceive? ........................

# month 11
## week 4

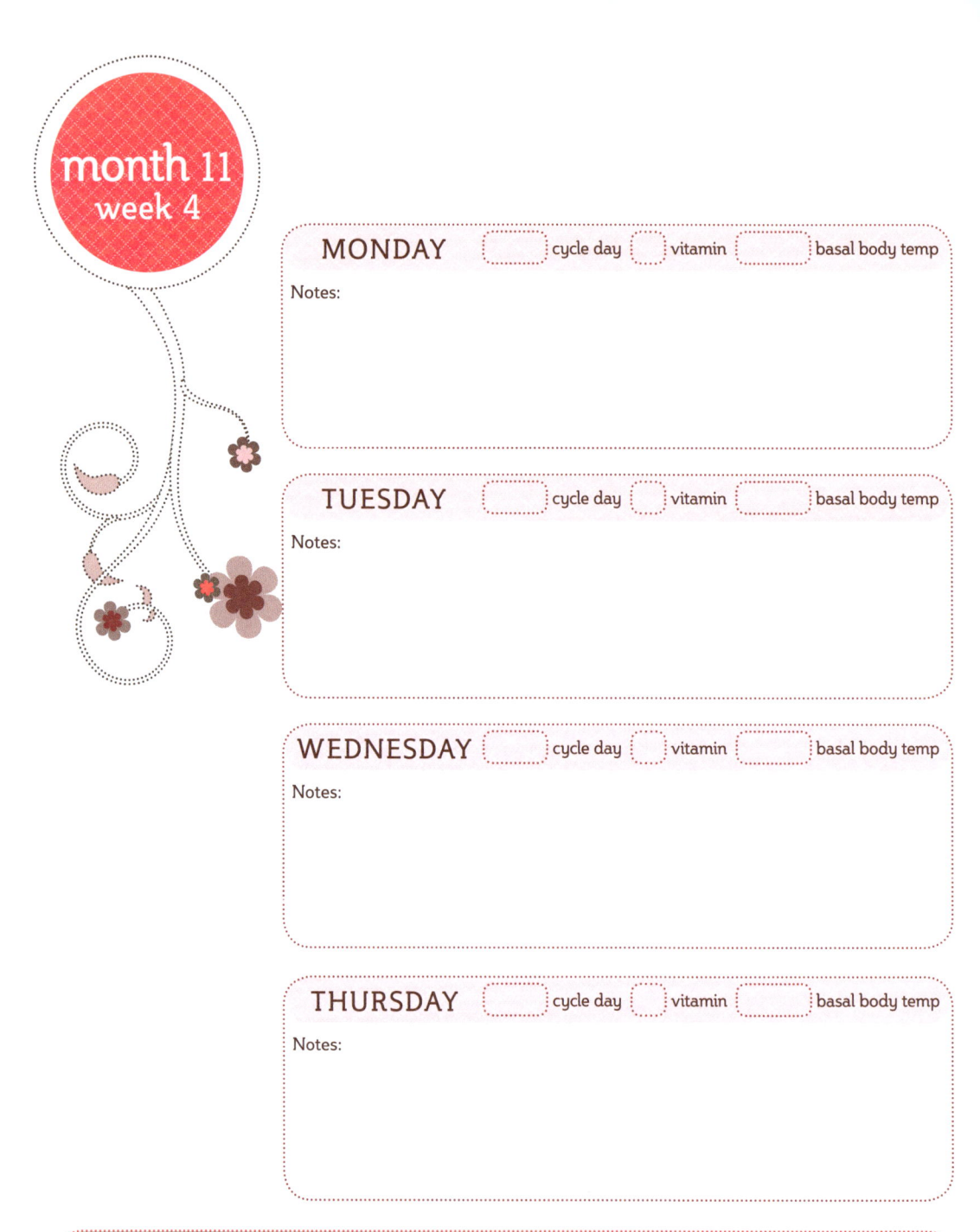

**MONDAY** — cycle day — vitamin — basal body temp
Notes:

**TUESDAY** — cycle day — vitamin — basal body temp
Notes:

**WEDNESDAY** — cycle day — vitamin — basal body temp
Notes:

**THURSDAY** — cycle day — vitamin — basal body temp
Notes:

## looking ahead to pregnancy: a special nine months of time together

Many couples see the nine months of pregnancy as a special time together. You and your husband will still be able to enjoy your relationship the way you did before, but now you'll also have a shared sense of excitement and anticipation about the next phase in your life. Be sure you keep celebrating your relationship even as you prepare for parenthood.

### FRIDAY
☐ cycle day ☐ vitamin ☐ basal body temp

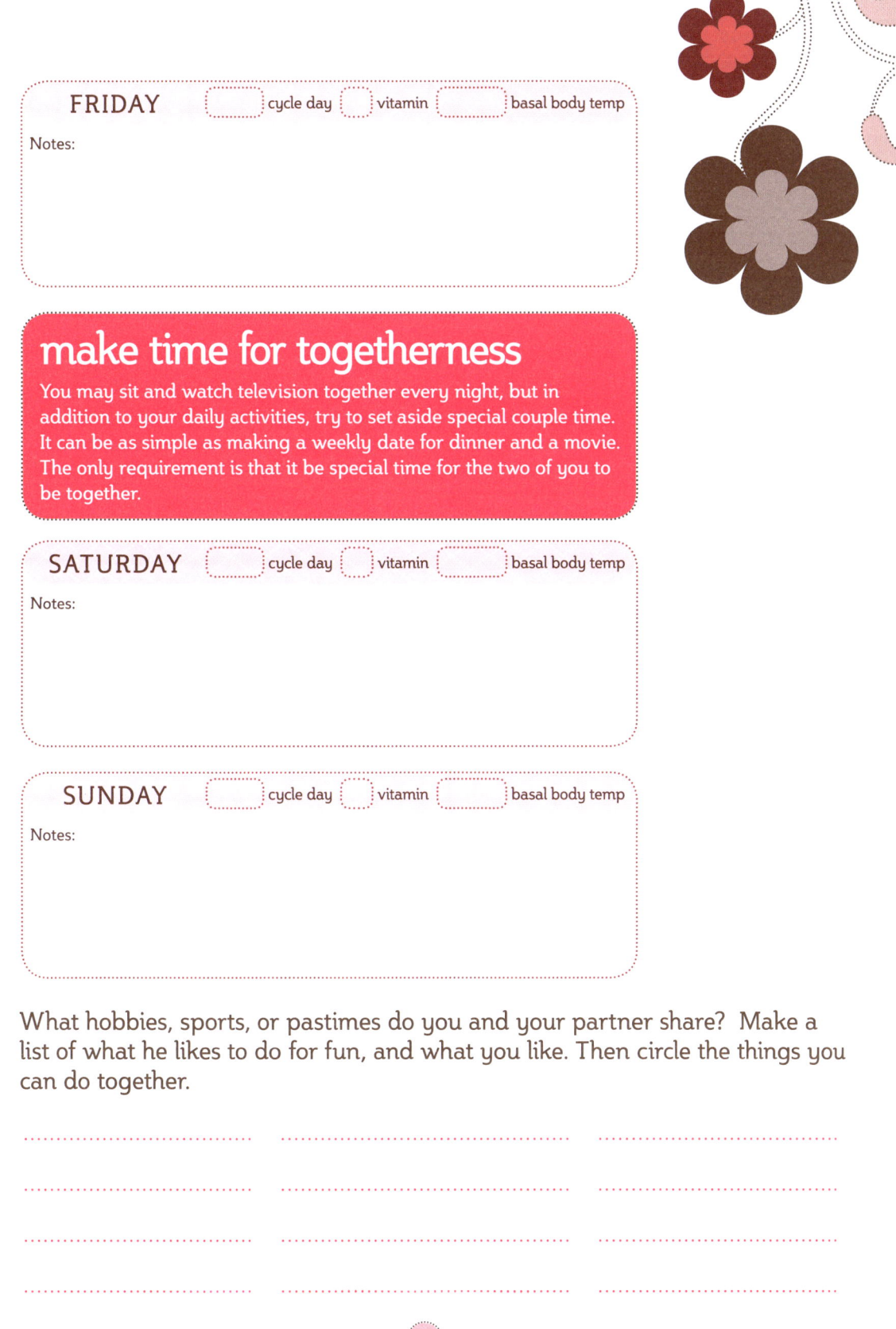

Notes:

## make time for togetherness
You may sit and watch television together every night, but in addition to your daily activities, try to set aside special couple time. It can be as simple as making a weekly date for dinner and a movie. The only requirement is that it be special time for the two of you to be together.

### SATURDAY
☐ cycle day ☐ vitamin ☐ basal body temp

Notes:

### SUNDAY
☐ cycle day ☐ vitamin ☐ basal body temp

Notes:

What hobbies, sports, or pastimes do you and your partner share? Make a list of what he likes to do for fun, and what you like. Then circle the things you can do together.

# month 12

## Preparing for Parenthood

You're probably so busy thinking about conception that you haven't had much of a chance to think about what comes after that: motherhood. Don't forget that being a mom is your goal, and conception and pregnancy are just one way to get there. No matter where you are in your journey right now, it's never too early to start thinking about parenthood.

What are you looking forward to most about being a mom? ................................................

................................................................................................................................................

What scares you about parenthood? ....................................................................................

................................................................................................................................................

Do most of your friends have children already, or will you be the first in your crowd?

................................................................................................................................................

How would you describe a terrific parent? ..........................................................................

................................................................................................................................................

What makes a bad parent? ....................................................................................................

................................................................................................................................................

What personality traits will make you a great mother? ....................................................

................................................................................................................................................

What do you think your biggest challenges will be? ..........................................................

................................................................................................................................................

Have you made a financial plan for parenthood?　　◯ Yes　　◯ No

## month 12 week 1

**MONDAY** — cycle day — vitamin — basal body temp
Notes:

**TUESDAY** — cycle day — vitamin — basal body temp
Notes:

**WEDNESDAY** — cycle day — vitamin — basal body temp
Notes:

**THURSDAY** — cycle day — vitamin — basal body temp
Notes:

## when two becomes three (or more)

For most couples, becoming parents will be a much bigger life change than getting married. Yet often a lot more thought goes into planning a wedding than preparing for parenthood. Talk with friends who have children. Read books about smart parenting and protecting your relationship once you become parents.

## looking ahead to pregnancy: practice parenting

There are childbirth education classes and classes in infant care, but there are few classes to teach you how to make the transition to parenthood with your partner. You can give yourself some practice by making an effort to be around children—of friends, family members, co-workers. Volunteer to baby-sit now in exchange for baby-sitting help later on after your baby is born.

**FRIDAY**  ◯ cycle day  ◯ vitamin  ◯ basal body temp

Notes:

**SATURDAY**  ◯ cycle day  ◯ vitamin  ◯ basal body temp

Notes:

**SUNDAY**  ◯ cycle day  ◯ vitamin  ◯ basal body temp

Notes:

What do you anticipate the biggest changes to your life will be when you have a baby? .................

................................................................................................................

................................................................................................................

................................................................................................................

Most of those changes will be joyous, but what might cause stress? ...................

................................................................................................................

................................................................................................................

................................................................................................................

## month 12
### week 2

**MONDAY** — cycle day — vitamin — basal body temp

Notes:

**TUESDAY** — cycle day — vitamin — basal body temp

Notes:

**WEDNESDAY** — cycle day — vitamin — basal body temp

Notes:

**THURSDAY** — cycle day — vitamin — basal body temp

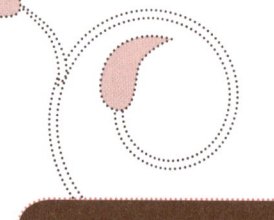

Notes:

# looking ahead to pregnancy: parenting dreams

Many women report vivid dreams during pregnancy, sometimes about parenting. You might dream, for instance, that you've left your baby on a bus . . . even though you'd never do that in real life. You might also have wonderful dreams about being a mom. All these dreams are a way for your subconscious to work out hopes and fears about parenthood.

Who are your parenting role models? ...........................................
..................................................................................................................

What was the best lesson you got from your own parents? ...............
..................................................................................................................

What do you plan to do differently from them? ...............................
..................................................................................................................

What will you try to replicate? ...........................................................
..................................................................................................................

**FRIDAY**  ⬚ cycle day  ⬚ vitamin  ⬚ basal body temp
Notes:

**SATURDAY**  ⬚ cycle day  ⬚ vitamin  ⬚ basal body temp
Notes:

**SUNDAY**  ⬚ cycle day  ⬚ vitamin  ⬚ basal body temp
Notes:

## you are not your mother

If you come from a challenging family background, you might think you want to do everything differently than your parents did. But instead of deciding what kind of parent you don't want to be, think about the kind of parent you hope to become.

# month 12
## week 3

**MONDAY** ⬚ cycle day ⬚ vitamin ⬚ basal body temp

Notes:

**TUESDAY** ⬚ cycle day ⬚ vitamin ⬚ basal body temp

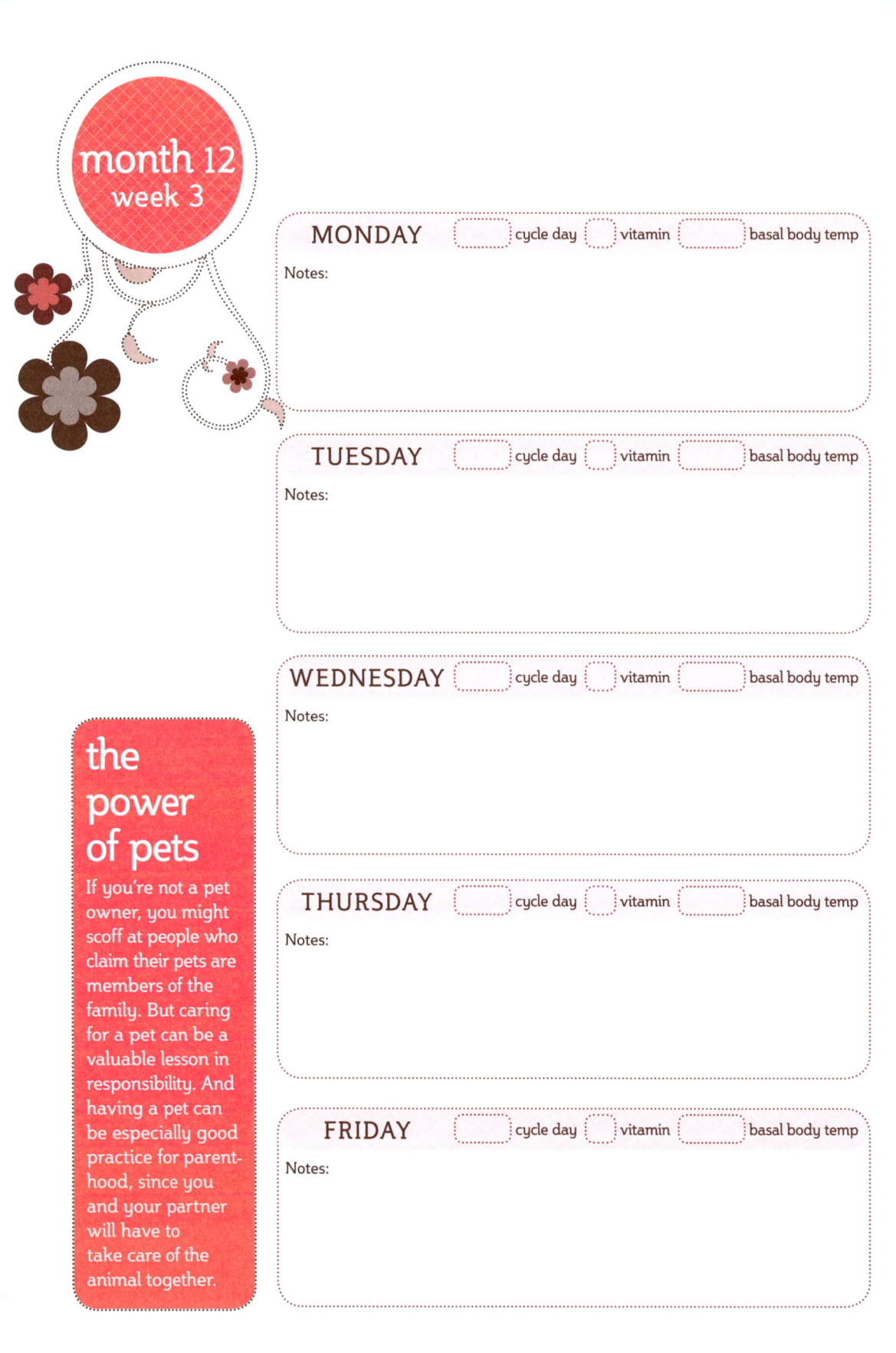

Notes:

**WEDNESDAY** ⬚ cycle day ⬚ vitamin ⬚ basal body temp

Notes:

**THURSDAY** ⬚ cycle day ⬚ vitamin ⬚ basal body temp

Notes:

**FRIDAY** ⬚ cycle day ⬚ vitamin ⬚ basal body temp

Notes:

## the power of pets

If you're not a pet owner, you might scoff at people who claim their pets are members of the family. But caring for a pet can be a valuable lesson in responsibility. And having a pet can be especially good practice for parenthood, since you and your partner will have to take care of the animal together.

# looking ahead to pregnancy: for cat owners

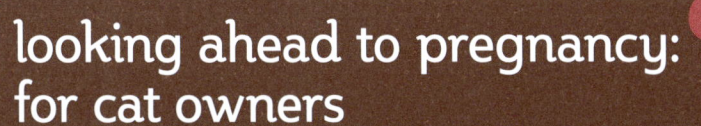

Cats can transmit a disease called toxoplasmosis, which can be dangerous to a developing infant. The disease-causing parasite is passed through feces, so pregnant women are advised not to change their cat's litter box. Consult your doctor for advice about what precautions to take, and whether or not you should have your pet tested for an active infection.

**SATURDAY** ⬚ cycle day ⬚ vitamin ⬚ basal body temp

Notes:

**SUNDAY** ⬚ cycle day ⬚ vitamin ⬚ basal body temp

Notes:

Have you and your partner ever cared for anything together—a niece or nephew, friend's child . . . a pet?

How did you work as a team?

# month 12
## week 4

**MONDAY** ☐ cycle day ☐ vitamin ☐ basal body temp

Notes:

## looking ahead to pregnancy: to stay at home or not?

Once you're pregnant, questions of whether to stay at home after the baby is born or go back to work are even more pressing. But you don't have to decide anything yet. Take your maternity leave, and then see when—or if—you're ready to return to work.

**TUESDAY** ☐ cycle day ☐ vitamin ☐ basal body temp

Notes:

**WEDNESDAY** ☐ cycle day ☐ vitamin ☐ basal body temp

Notes:

**THURSDAY** — cycle day — vitamin — basal body temp

Notes:

## conceptual careers

You're probably planning to keep working while you're trying to conceive, and through most of your pregnancy. Now is a good time to assess the family-friendly benefits offered by your employer. Besides prenatal care benefits and maternity leave policies, look into what kinds of fertility treatment and adoption funds your company offers.

**FRIDAY** — cycle day — vitamin — basal body temp

Notes:

**SATURDAY** — cycle day — vitamin — basal body temp

Notes:

**SUNDAY** — cycle day — vitamin — basal body temp

Notes:

How important is your work to your identity?

Is your financial contribution crucial to your family?

If you didn't have to worry about money, would you keep working?

How much time do you hope to take off once the baby is born?

# when you need a little help...

If you've reached this point in the journal after filling out your twelve months of calendar pages, you're probably worried that it's taking too long to get pregnant. No need to panic, but you're right not to wait any longer before seeking some help. Experts recommend that couples consult a doctor after a year of unsuccessful trying—meaning regular sexual intercourse without contraceptives. (For women over age thirty-five, the advice is to consult a doctor after six months.) One in six couples will encounter some fertility challenges, but the vast majority of them will become pregnant. It just might take a little longer.

So far we've avoided talking about the dreaded "biological clock." Women can and do become pregnant naturally at all ages (at least, all ages before menopause), but there's no denying that it does become more difficult as women get older. A woman's fertility begins declining in her twenties, and becomes more precarious after age thirty-five; by the forties it's much more difficult to conceive naturally. Here are some numbers to put it in perspective: If you're in your early twenties, you have about a 25 percent chance of conceiving every month, and it will only take an average of four or five months to become pregnant; by the late twenties the average is six or seven months. By your thirties there's a 10 to 15 percent chance of conceiving each

# when you need help

month, with an average seven to twelve months to conceive. After age 40—well, after age 40 you only have a 5 percent chance of conceiving naturally each month. But that still doesn't mean you can't become a mom.

While many people believe that infertility is a woman's problem, that's simply not true. Infertility affects as many men as women, and when a couple is having problems conceiving, it's estimated that about one-third of the time it's due to a problem with the woman, one-third of the time to a problem with the man, and the remaining third of fertility problems are either due to a combination of male and female factors, or to "unexplained infertility" (meaning that no cause can be found).

Whatever the reason, you've now reached the point in your parenthood journey where you need some advice. Start by talking to your regular gynecologist. If the problem is something simple, he or she may be able to deal with it quickly.

While you can't change your age, there are many other things that may be standing in the way of pregnancy that you can take care of fairly easily. Sometimes, for instance, both members of a couple have schedules so hectic that it's almost impossible to make love at the right time of the cycle for months at a time. Here are some common roadblocks on the path to pregnancy:

## diagnosis: irregular ovulation

If you tried charting your periods and discovered that your cycle varies by more than a few days, it may indicate that you're not ovulating regularly. A normal menstrual cycle is between twenty-three and thirty-five days long. Your period may be twenty-seven days one month, and twenty-nine days another—that's perfectly normal. But if your cycle is shorter than twenty-three days, longer than thirty-five, or sometimes skips a month completely, you may need help to get ovulation on track.

**treatment:** Your doctor may prescribe a drug such as clomiphene citrate (marketed under names such as Clomid and Serophene) to boost your ovulation. For many women, this is all that's needed to achieve pregnancy.

**23 to 35 days**
The length of a normal menstrual cycle.

### diagnosis: polycystic ovary syndrome (PCOS)

This disorder, a common cause of female infertility, occurs when the ovaries produce too much of the male hormones, such as testosterone. The resulting hormone imbalance interferes with normal ovulation. For more than three-quarters of women with PCOS, the first symptom is an absent, irregular, or overly long (40 days or more) cycle. Other symptoms can include extra hair growth (including hair on the face, chest, lower abdomen, and thighs), acne, and weight gain.

**treatment:** For some women, weight loss and lifestyle changes alone can minimize PCOS symptoms and regulate ovulation. Doctors may prescribe clomiphene citrate to help women with PCOS ovulate. Sometimes the diabetes drug metformin (Glucophage) is added for women with PCOS who don't respond to clomiphene alone.

### diagnosis: obstructions

In women, past or present sexually transmitted infections—often without symptoms—can cause scarring in the reproductive organs, making it difficult for a fertilized egg to get to the uterus. Endometriosis, and uterine fibroids or polyps can also make it physically impossible for the egg to be properly released and travel to the uterus. In men, scarring from sexually transmitted diseases can block the path that sperm travel to reach the egg.

**treatment:** Surgical procedures can clear the blockages in both women and men. If the pathway can't be cleared in either partner, it may be necessary to bypass the blockage by going on to a procedure like in vitro fertilization (IVF—more on that later) to achieve pregnancy.

And two challenges that may affect *him* alone:

### diagnosis: varicoceles

This is the most common cause of male infertility. Varicoceles are varicose veins in the scrotum, and they're surprisingly common—an estimated 15 percent of men

> Experts recommend that couples under 35 consult a doctor after a year of unsuccessful trying—meaning regular sexual intercourse without contraceptives.

## when you need help

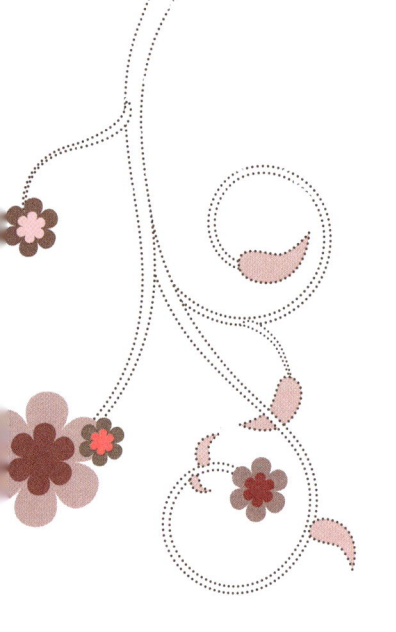

have this condition, although many of them aren't aware of it. Small varicoceles probably won't interfere with sperm quantity or quality, but larger ones may cause problems. The enlarged or dilated veins can cause blood to pool, which raises the temperature of the scrotum and affects sperm production.

**treatment:** Varicoceles can be repaired with a minor microsurgical procedure.

### diagnosis: heat

The testicles are outside the body because the enzymes required to produce sperm are extremely sensitive to heat. Doctors often advise men who are trying to get a partner pregnant to avoid things that would heat up the testicles, including wearing tight-fitting underwear or exercise shorts, soaking in very hot baths, sitting for hours in a car or truck, or bike riding for long distances. Studies have also found that the heat from laptop computers, electric blankets, and water beds may affect a man's fertility. And new research is linking cell phone radiation with fertility problems in men, too.

**treatment:** For most men, the activities listed above will probably not affect sperm count or quality enough to prevent conception. But for couples having conception challenges, turning down the heat can sometimes make a difference.

**85%**
The number of patients who can be treated successfully by a reproductive endocrinologist with simple medication or surgical repair.

If your problem can't be diagnosed, or can't be handled simply, you'll probably be referred to a reproductive endocrinologist—a fertility specialist. You can get a recommendation from your regular doctor, or from a friend who has been treated for infertility (and don't we all have friends who have?). Bring your partner to your first visit, as the doctor will be taking a complete history from both of you.

Visiting a reproductive endocrinologist doesn't mean you're starting down a path that necessarily ends in high-tech treatments like embryo freezing and in vitro fertilization. These super-high-tech procedures might get all the publicity, but it's estimated that 85 percent of patients can be treated with simple medication or surgical repair.

Fertility testing for men starts with a little plastic cup and some privacy. The sperm sample is then evaluated for the number of sperm (sperm count), the shape and physical appearance of the sperm (sperm morphology), and the way the sperm move (sperm motility). A problem with any of these factors can impede conception. Believe it or not, in a typical ejaculate—about one teaspoon—there are 250 million sperm released. A low sperm count—defined as 20 million or fewer sperm per milliliter of ejaculate—doesn't mean pregnancy won't happen, just that it might take longer.

Since it only takes one sperm to fertilize an egg, you might wonder why so many are needed for fertility. Of the millions of sperm released from an ejaculation, only hundreds make it as far as the fallopian tubes. The rest perish in the female reproductive tract after releasing an enzyme that helps clear the pathway to the egg so that a single sperm can penetrate it.

Today, there are few men who can't go on to biologically father a child. Even in men with very low sperm counts or those with high numbers of abnormal sperm, technology can help. In a process called intracytoplasmic sperm injection (ICSI), a single sperm cell can be injected into the egg, giving the sperm a boost after analysis has identified a problem. Today fertilization may be possible with even the worst semen analysis results.

For women, a "fertility workup" may involve a number of different tests, including:

- A cervical culture to detect active infections, such as sexually transmitted diseases
- A blood test to determine levels of fertility-predicting reproductive hormones
- Hysterosalpingogram, an X-ray of the pelvic region to reveal blockage or scarring
- Pelvic ultrasound to determine the number of undeveloped egg follicles in the ovaries
- A cervical mucus swab, done post-coitally, to see if sperm can swim normally in the fluid

## when you need help

If a specific fertility problem can't be diagnosed or treated, or medications alone don't succeed in producing a pregnancy, the next step may be IUI—intrauterine insemination. In this form of artificial insemination, a man's semen is "washed" to separate the sperm from the seminal fluid, increasing the concentration. Using a small catheter, the doctor then inserts the sperm high up in the woman's cervix or into the uterus itself, optimizing the chance for conception.

Finally, when all these less invasive (and less expensive) methods have not produced a pregnancy, a reproductive endocrinologist may recommend that a couple progress to in vitro fertilization (IVF). This technology is a fertility specialist's most potent offering, and has enabled hundreds of thousands of couples to become biological parents.

An IVF cycle generally starts with a round of drugs to suppress a woman's own natural menstrual cycle, allowing the doctor to control the timing of events. Next comes medication to stimulate the growth of the follicles, so they produce many mature eggs rather than the single egg produced during a natural cycle. The number and size of the follicles are carefully monitored with blood tests and ultrasounds, and when the follicles reach the right size, ovulation is induced. About a day and a half later, the eggs are "retrieved" and taken to the lab, where they are fertilized with sperm. The fertilized eggs are left to grow in the laboratory for two to five days. The resulting embryos are then graded, and one or two of the best ones are transferred into the woman's uterus. After two weeks, a blood test determines whether pregnancy has occurred.

Scientists are constantly making improvements to IVF to ensure that a higher percentage of cycles are successful. There are new cultures being developed for growing the fertilized eggs, new ways to determine which embryos are most likely to result in a successful pregnancy, and new ways of harvesting immature eggs and allowing them to develop in the lab (minimizing the need for many fertility drugs). All of these innovations, and more to come, will help science get closer to the ideal of enabling every couple who wants to become biological parents to achieve their goal.

> Visiting a reproductive endocrinologist doesn't necessarily mean you're starting down a path that ends in high-tech treatments like embryo freezing and in vitro fertilization.

# Alphabet Soup

The acronyms tossed around in fertility clinics can be confusing. Here's how to break the code and learn more about treatment.

**ART:** Assisted reproductive technology
A phrase to describe any treatments that involve handling human eggs or embryos.

**CASA:** Computer-assisted semen analysis
A laboratory technique to precisely measure and study sperm motion when male infertility is suspected.

**CCCT:** Clomiphene citrate challenge test
A blood test to measure FSH (see below) taken on days three and 10 of the menstrual cycle. Clomiphene citrate (marketed under name brands such as Clomid, Serophene) is taken on days five through nine to induce ovulation.

**EEJ:** Electroejaculation
A procedure that involves electrically stimulating tissue near a man's prostate to cause ejaculation.

**FSH:** Follicle stimulating hormone
A hormone produced by the pituitary gland (and sometimes given by injection). FSH stimulates the growth of the follicle surrounding an egg.

**GnRH:** Gonadotropin releasing hormone
A hormone secreted by the hypothalamus (an area of the brain that controls reproduction and other actions) that prompts the pituitary gland to release FSH and LH (see right) into the bloodstream.

**hCG:** Human chorionic gonadotropin
A hormone produced by the placenta that is measured in common pregnancy tests. It may also be injected to stimulate ovulation and maturation of eggs.

**HSG:** Hysterosalpingogram
An X-ray procedure to determine whether the fallopian tubes are open and to check for abnormalities in the uterus.

**ICSI:** Intracytoplasmic sperm injection
A procedure in which a single sperm is injected directly into an egg to help spur fertilization, used primarily in cases of male infertility.

**IUI:** Intrauterine insemination
A form of artificial insemination in which sperm that has been washed free of seminal fluid to increase the chance of fertilization is inserted directly into the uterus.

**IVF:** In vitro fertilization
A procedure in which an egg and sperm are combined in the laboratory to facilitate fertilization. Resulting embryos are transferred to a woman's uterus.

**LH:** Luteinizing hormone
Produced by the pituitary gland, this hormone normally causes a woman to ovulate and her eggs to mature.

**MESA:** Microepididymal sperm aspiration
A procedure for collecting sperm from men whose reproductive ducts are blocked, usually as a result of a vasectomy or absence of vas deferens (the tubes that carry sperm to the urethra).

**OHSS:** Ovarian hyper-stimulation syndrome
A potentially life-threatening condition characterized by enlargement of the ovaries, fluid retention and weight gain that may occur when the ovaries are overstimulated during assisted reproduction.

**PESA:** Percutaneous epididymal sperm aspiration
A procedure in which a needle is inserted into the gland that carries sperm from the testicle to the vas deferens in order to extract sperm for an IVF procedure.

**PGD:** Preimplantation genetic diagnosis
A test in which one or two cells are removed from an embryo and screened for genetic abnormalities.

**TESE:** Testicular sperm extraction
Surgery to remove testicular tissue and collect living sperm for use in an IVF or ICSI procedure.

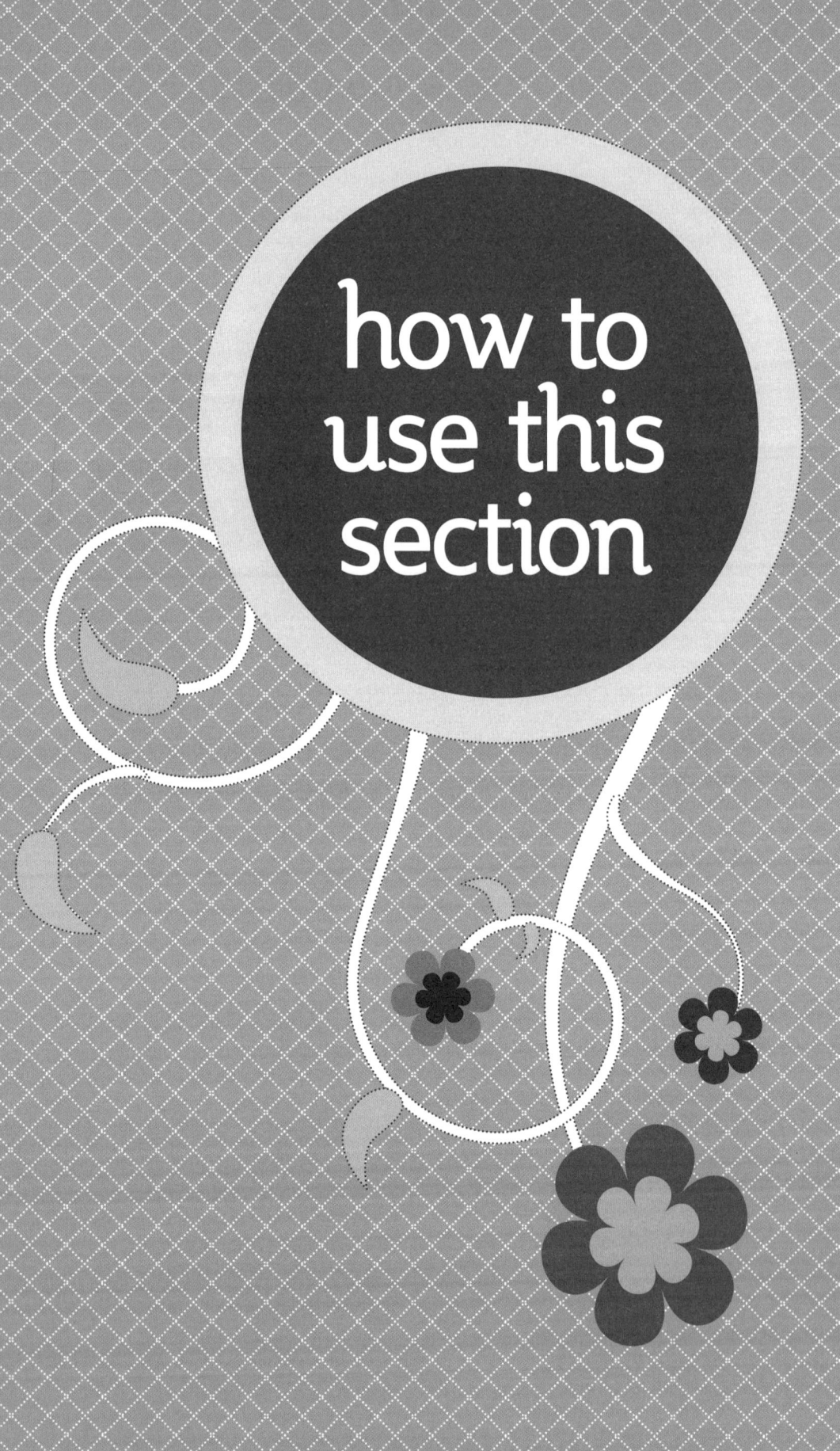

# how to use this section

The calendar pages for you to fill out in this section are somewhat different from the calendar pages that came before, because fertility treatments, including in vitro fertilization (IVF), require a different kind of tracking. Rather than trying to pinpoint ovulation each cycle, women who are undergoing fertility treatments need to keep track of various medications—oral and injectable—that will help them become mothers. And it's important that some of the medications be taken at exactly the same time each day. So these calendar pages give you space to organize and track your prescriptions, to ensure that you take what you need, when you need it.

If you've decided to try IVF, your ovulatory cycle will be artificially regulated and manipulated to promote conception. For about two weeks before the IVF cycle actually begins (weeks one and two on the following Fertility Treatment cycle pages), you'll be taking medications to suppress your natural cycle. After tests to determine whether the suppression was successful, the "real" IVF cycle begins, and you'll be given medications—usually injections—to stimulate the ovaries (weeks three and four on the following Fertility Treatment cycle pages). If all goes well with this phase, the eggs will be harvested around day 12 and fertilized in the lab. The fertilized eggs will be left to develop in a special lab culture for three to five days, and then transferred into the uterus. After that, it's a two-week wait (weeks five and six on the following Fertility Treatment cycle pages) to find out whether the embryos implanted . . . and whether or not you're pregnant.

So in this section of the journal, we've given you six weeks of calendar pages to keep track of your medications and doctor's recommendations for two cycles. And then, for those stressful two weeks before your pregnancy test, we've given you things to think about and blank pages to write on, in the hopes that getting your feelings on paper will help make those two weeks go faster . . . or at least easier. Good luck!

## fertility treatment CYCLE 1

# Week 1

**DATE** .................... ( ) cycle day ( ) vitamin

APPOINTMENTS / DOCTOR'S ORDERS

**MEDICATIONS**

Oral — Time — Name — Amount

Inj. — Time — Name — Amount

**DATE** .................... ( ) cycle day ( ) vitamin

APPOINTMENTS / DOCTOR'S ORDERS

**MEDICATIONS**

Oral — Time — Name — Amount

Inj. — Time — Name — Amount

**DATE** .................... ( ) cycle day ( ) vitamin

APPOINTMENTS / DOCTOR'S ORDERS

**MEDICATIONS**

Oral — Time — Name — Amount

Inj. — Time — Name — Amount

## DATE ........................  ( ) cycle day  ( ) vitamin

### APPOINTMENTS / DOCTOR'S ORDERS

## MEDICATIONS

| Oral | Time | Name | Amount |
|---|---|---|---|
| ( ) | | | |
| ( ) | | | |

| Inj. | Time | Name | Amount |
|---|---|---|---|
| ( ) | | | |
| ( ) | | | |
| ( ) | | | |
| ( ) | | | |
| ( ) | | | |

---

## DATE ........................  ( ) cycle day  ( ) vitamin

### APPOINTMENTS / DOCTOR'S ORDERS

## MEDICATIONS

| Oral | Time | Name | Amount |
|---|---|---|---|
| ( ) | | | |
| ( ) | | | |

| Inj. | Time | Name | Amount |
|---|---|---|---|
| ( ) | | | |
| ( ) | | | |
| ( ) | | | |
| ( ) | | | |
| ( ) | | | |

---

## DATE ........................  ( ) cycle day  ( ) vitamin

### APPOINTMENTS / DOCTOR'S ORDERS

## MEDICATIONS

| Oral | Time | Name | Amount |
|---|---|---|---|
| ( ) | | | |
| ( ) | | | |

| Inj. | Time | Name | Amount |
|---|---|---|---|
| ( ) | | | |
| ( ) | | | |
| ( ) | | | |
| ( ) | | | |
| ( ) | | | |

---

## DATE ........................  ( ) cycle day  ( ) vitamin

### APPOINTMENTS / DOCTOR'S ORDERS

## MEDICATIONS

| Oral | Time | Name | Amount |
|---|---|---|---|
| ( ) | | | |
| ( ) | | | |

| Inj. | Time | Name | Amount |
|---|---|---|---|
| ( ) | | | |
| ( ) | | | |
| ( ) | | | |
| ( ) | | | |
| ( ) | | | |

# fertility treatment CYCLE 1

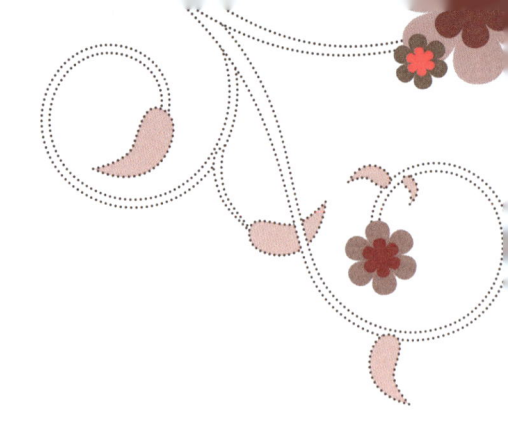

# Week 2

**DATE** ............................ ( ) cycle day ( ) vitamin

APPOINTMENTS / DOCTOR'S ORDERS

**MEDICATIONS**

| Oral | Time | Name | Amount |
|---|---|---|---|

| Inj. | Time | Name | Amount |
|---|---|---|---|

---

**DATE** ............................ ( ) cycle day ( ) vitamin

APPOINTMENTS / DOCTOR'S ORDERS

**MEDICATIONS**

| Oral | Time | Name | Amount |
|---|---|---|---|

| Inj. | Time | Name | Amount |
|---|---|---|---|

---

**DATE** ............................ ( ) cycle day ( ) vitamin

APPOINTMENTS / DOCTOR'S ORDERS

**MEDICATIONS**

| Oral | Time | Name | Amount |
|---|---|---|---|

| Inj. | Time | Name | Amount |
|---|---|---|---|

# DATE ............  ( ) cycle day ( ) vitamin

## APPOINTMENTS / DOCTOR'S ORDERS

## MEDICATIONS

| Oral | Time | Name | Amount |
|------|------|------|--------|
| ○ | | | |
| ○ | | | |

| Inj. | Time | Name | Amount |
|------|------|------|--------|
| ○ | | | |
| ○ | | | |
| ○ | | | |
| ○ | | | |
| ○ | | | |

---

# DATE ............  ( ) cycle day ( ) vitamin

## APPOINTMENTS / DOCTOR'S ORDERS

## MEDICATIONS

| Oral | Time | Name | Amount |
|------|------|------|--------|
| ○ | | | |
| ○ | | | |

| Inj. | Time | Name | Amount |
|------|------|------|--------|
| ○ | | | |
| ○ | | | |
| ○ | | | |
| ○ | | | |
| ○ | | | |

---

# DATE ............  ( ) cycle day ( ) vitamin

## APPOINTMENTS / DOCTOR'S ORDERS

## MEDICATIONS

| Oral | Time | Name | Amount |
|------|------|------|--------|
| ○ | | | |
| ○ | | | |

| Inj. | Time | Name | Amount |
|------|------|------|--------|
| ○ | | | |
| ○ | | | |
| ○ | | | |
| ○ | | | |
| ○ | | | |

---

# DATE ............  ( ) cycle day ( ) vitamin

## APPOINTMENTS / DOCTOR'S ORDERS

## MEDICATIONS

| Oral | Time | Name | Amount |
|------|------|------|--------|
| ○ | | | |
| ○ | | | |

| Inj. | Time | Name | Amount |
|------|------|------|--------|
| ○ | | | |
| ○ | | | |
| ○ | | | |
| ○ | | | |
| ○ | | | |

**fertility treatment CYCLE 1**

# Week 3

| DATE .................... ( ) cycle day ( ) vitamin | MEDICATIONS |
|---|---|
| APPOINTMENTS / DOCTOR'S ORDERS | Oral  Time  Name  Amount |
|  | Inj.  Time  Name  Amount |

| DATE .................... ( ) cycle day ( ) vitamin | MEDICATIONS |
|---|---|
| APPOINTMENTS / DOCTOR'S ORDERS | Oral  Time  Name  Amount |
|  | Inj.  Time  Name  Amount |

| DATE .................... ( ) cycle day ( ) vitamin | MEDICATIONS |
|---|---|
| APPOINTMENTS / DOCTOR'S ORDERS | Oral  Time  Name  Amount |
|  | Inj.  Time  Name  Amount |

## DATE ............  ◯ cycle day  ◯ vitamin

### APPOINTMENTS / DOCTOR'S ORDERS

### MEDICATIONS

| Oral | Time | Name | Amount |
|---|---|---|---|
| ◯ | | | |
| ◯ | | | |

| Inj. | Time | Name | Amount |
|---|---|---|---|
| ◯ | | | |
| ◯ | | | |
| ◯ | | | |
| ◯ | | | |
| ◯ | | | |

---

## DATE ............  ◯ cycle day  ◯ vitamin

### APPOINTMENTS / DOCTOR'S ORDERS

### MEDICATIONS

| Oral | Time | Name | Amount |
|---|---|---|---|
| ◯ | | | |
| ◯ | | | |

| Inj. | Time | Name | Amount |
|---|---|---|---|
| ◯ | | | |
| ◯ | | | |
| ◯ | | | |
| ◯ | | | |
| ◯ | | | |

---

## DATE ............  ◯ cycle day  ◯ vitamin

### APPOINTMENTS / DOCTOR'S ORDERS

### MEDICATIONS

| Oral | Time | Name | Amount |
|---|---|---|---|
| ◯ | | | |
| ◯ | | | |

| Inj. | Time | Name | Amount |
|---|---|---|---|
| ◯ | | | |
| ◯ | | | |
| ◯ | | | |
| ◯ | | | |
| ◯ | | | |

---

## DATE ............  ◯ cycle day  ◯ vitamin

### APPOINTMENTS / DOCTOR'S ORDERS

### MEDICATIONS

| Oral | Time | Name | Amount |
|---|---|---|---|
| ◯ | | | |
| ◯ | | | |

| Inj. | Time | Name | Amount |
|---|---|---|---|
| ◯ | | | |
| ◯ | | | |
| ◯ | | | |
| ◯ | | | |
| ◯ | | | |

**fertility treatment CYCLE 1**

# Week 4

| DATE | ◯ cycle day ◯ vitamin |
|---|---|
| APPOINTMENTS / DOCTOR'S ORDERS | |

**MEDICATIONS**

Oral   Time   Name   Amount

Inj.   Time   Name   Amount

---

| DATE | ◯ cycle day ◯ vitamin |
|---|---|
| APPOINTMENTS / DOCTOR'S ORDERS | |

**MEDICATIONS**

Oral   Time   Name   Amount

Inj.   Time   Name   Amount

---

| DATE | ◯ cycle day ◯ vitamin |
|---|---|
| APPOINTMENTS / DOCTOR'S ORDERS | |

**MEDICATIONS**

Oral   Time   Name   Amount

Inj.   Time   Name   Amount

## DATE ............ ◯ cycle day ◯ vitamin

### APPOINTMENTS / DOCTOR'S ORDERS

### MEDICATIONS

| Oral | Time | Name | Amount |
|---|---|---|---|
| ◯ | | | |
| ◯ | | | |

| Inj. | Time | Name | Amount |
|---|---|---|---|
| ◯ | | | |
| ◯ | | | |
| ◯ | | | |
| ◯ | | | |
| ◯ | | | |

---

## DATE ............ ◯ cycle day ◯ vitamin

### APPOINTMENTS / DOCTOR'S ORDERS

### MEDICATIONS

| Oral | Time | Name | Amount |
|---|---|---|---|
| ◯ | | | |
| ◯ | | | |

| Inj. | Time | Name | Amount |
|---|---|---|---|
| ◯ | | | |
| ◯ | | | |
| ◯ | | | |
| ◯ | | | |
| ◯ | | | |

---

## DATE ............ ◯ cycle day ◯ vitamin

### APPOINTMENTS / DOCTOR'S ORDERS

### MEDICATIONS

| Oral | Time | Name | Amount |
|---|---|---|---|
| ◯ | | | |
| ◯ | | | |

| Inj. | Time | Name | Amount |
|---|---|---|---|
| ◯ | | | |
| ◯ | | | |
| ◯ | | | |
| ◯ | | | |
| ◯ | | | |

---

## DATE ............ ◯ cycle day ◯ vitamin

### APPOINTMENTS / DOCTOR'S ORDERS

### MEDICATIONS

| Oral | Time | Name | Amount |
|---|---|---|---|
| ◯ | | | |
| ◯ | | | |

| Inj. | Time | Name | Amount |
|---|---|---|---|
| ◯ | | | |
| ◯ | | | |
| ◯ | | | |
| ◯ | | | |
| ◯ | | | |

# fertility treatment CYCLE 1

# Week 5

| DATE | cycle day | vitamin | MEDICATIONS |
|---|---|---|---|

APPOINTMENTS / DOCTOR'S ORDERS

Oral | Time | Name | Amount

Inj. | Time | Name | Amount

| DATE | cycle day | vitamin | MEDICATIONS |
|---|---|---|---|

APPOINTMENTS / DOCTOR'S ORDERS

Oral | Time | Name | Amount

Inj. | Time | Name | Amount

| DATE | cycle day | vitamin | MEDICATIONS |
|---|---|---|---|

APPOINTMENTS / DOCTOR'S ORDERS

Oral | Time | Name | Amount

Inj. | Time | Name | Amount

| DATE ..................... | ⬭ cycle day ⬭ vitamin | MEDICATIONS | | | |
|---|---|---|---|---|---|
| APPOINTMENTS / DOCTOR'S ORDERS | | Oral | Time | Name | Amount |
| | | ⬭ | | | |
| | | ⬭ | | | |
| | | Inj. | Time | Name | Amount |
| | | ⬭ | | | |
| | | ⬭ | | | |
| | | ⬭ | | | |
| | | ⬭ | | | |
| | | ⬭ | | | |

| DATE ..................... | ⬭ cycle day ⬭ vitamin | MEDICATIONS | | | |
|---|---|---|---|---|---|
| APPOINTMENTS / DOCTOR'S ORDERS | | Oral | Time | Name | Amount |
| | | ⬭ | | | |
| | | ⬭ | | | |
| | | Inj. | Time | Name | Amount |
| | | ⬭ | | | |
| | | ⬭ | | | |
| | | ⬭ | | | |
| | | ⬭ | | | |
| | | ⬭ | | | |

| DATE ..................... | ⬭ cycle day ⬭ vitamin | MEDICATIONS | | | |
|---|---|---|---|---|---|
| APPOINTMENTS / DOCTOR'S ORDERS | | Oral | Time | Name | Amount |
| | | ⬭ | | | |
| | | ⬭ | | | |
| | | Inj. | Time | Name | Amount |
| | | ⬭ | | | |
| | | ⬭ | | | |
| | | ⬭ | | | |
| | | ⬭ | | | |
| | | ⬭ | | | |

| DATE ..................... | ⬭ cycle day ⬭ vitamin | MEDICATIONS | | | |
|---|---|---|---|---|---|
| APPOINTMENTS / DOCTOR'S ORDERS | | Oral | Time | Name | Amount |
| | | ⬭ | | | |
| | | ⬭ | | | |
| | | Inj. | Time | Name | Amount |
| | | ⬭ | | | |
| | | ⬭ | | | |
| | | ⬭ | | | |
| | | ⬭ | | | |
| | | ⬭ | | | |

## fertility treatment CYCLE 1

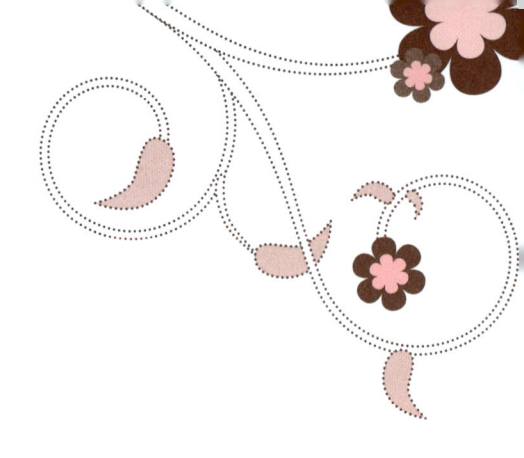

# Week 6

**DATE** .................................... ( ) cycle day ( ) vitamin

**APPOINTMENTS / DOCTOR'S ORDERS**

**MEDICATIONS**

| Oral | Time | Name | Amount |
|---|---|---|---|
| ( ) | | | |
| ( ) | | | |

| Inj. | Time | Name | Amount |
|---|---|---|---|
| ( ) | | | |
| ( ) | | | |
| ( ) | | | |
| ( ) | | | |
| ( ) | | | |

**DATE** .................................... ( ) cycle day ( ) vitamin

**APPOINTMENTS / DOCTOR'S ORDERS**

**MEDICATIONS**

| Oral | Time | Name | Amount |
|---|---|---|---|
| ( ) | | | |
| ( ) | | | |

| Inj. | Time | Name | Amount |
|---|---|---|---|
| ( ) | | | |
| ( ) | | | |
| ( ) | | | |
| ( ) | | | |
| ( ) | | | |

**DATE** .................................... ( ) cycle day ( ) vitamin

**APPOINTMENTS / DOCTOR'S ORDERS**

**MEDICATIONS**

| Oral | Time | Name | Amount |
|---|---|---|---|
| ( ) | | | |
| ( ) | | | |

| Inj. | Time | Name | Amount |
|---|---|---|---|
| ( ) | | | |
| ( ) | | | |
| ( ) | | | |
| ( ) | | | |
| ( ) | | | |

## DATE ........... ( ) cycle day ( ) vitamin

### APPOINTMENTS / DOCTOR'S ORDERS

### MEDICATIONS

| Oral | Time | Name | Amount |
|---|---|---|---|
| ○ | | | |
| ○ | | | |

| Inj. | Time | Name | Amount |
|---|---|---|---|
| ○ | | | |
| ○ | | | |
| ○ | | | |
| ○ | | | |
| ○ | | | |

---

## DATE ........... ( ) cycle day ( ) vitamin

### APPOINTMENTS / DOCTOR'S ORDERS

### MEDICATIONS

| Oral | Time | Name | Amount |
|---|---|---|---|
| ○ | | | |
| ○ | | | |

| Inj. | Time | Name | Amount |
|---|---|---|---|
| ○ | | | |
| ○ | | | |
| ○ | | | |
| ○ | | | |
| ○ | | | |

---

## DATE ........... ( ) cycle day ( ) vitamin

### APPOINTMENTS / DOCTOR'S ORDERS

### MEDICATIONS

| Oral | Time | Name | Amount |
|---|---|---|---|
| ○ | | | |
| ○ | | | |

| Inj. | Time | Name | Amount |
|---|---|---|---|
| ○ | | | |
| ○ | | | |
| ○ | | | |
| ○ | | | |
| ○ | | | |

---

## DATE ........... ( ) cycle day ( ) vitamin

### APPOINTMENTS / DOCTOR'S ORDERS

### MEDICATIONS

| Oral | Time | Name | Amount |
|---|---|---|---|
| ○ | | | |
| ○ | | | |

| Inj. | Time | Name | Amount |
|---|---|---|---|
| ○ | | | |
| ○ | | | |
| ○ | | | |
| ○ | | | |
| ○ | | | |

**fertility treatment CYCLE 1**

# Getting through the Dreaded TWW (Two-Week Wait)

Trying to get pregnant can seem like an endless progression of things to wait for. When you were trying to get pregnant through natural conception, you waited to see if you got your period each month. When you started going for fertility treatment, you waited for the results of every new test or attempt. And now you're doing IVF. First you have to wait to see if you produce enough eggs, then you have to wait to see if your eggs are fertilized by your partner's sperm, then you have to wait and find out if you produced any good embryos, and then, after you finally have embryos implanted, comes the worst wait of all: the two-week wait after the embryos are implanted before you find out if you're pregnant. These two weeks can seem endless.

But there are ways to make the wait bearable, to turn the dread into joyous anticipation of the life you hope is growing within. It's time to start thinking of yourself as a mother-to-be, because you will be a mother: if not sooner, then later. Instead of dwelling on the waiting, try to think about the hopes and dreams you have for your family-to-be.

Use these pages to help you manage the two-week wait. Think of the journal as a kind of prebaby book, where you can write down your thoughts about trying to get pregnant. Someday you may want to add these pages into your child's actual baby book.

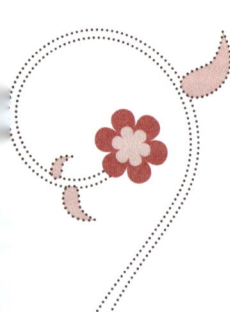

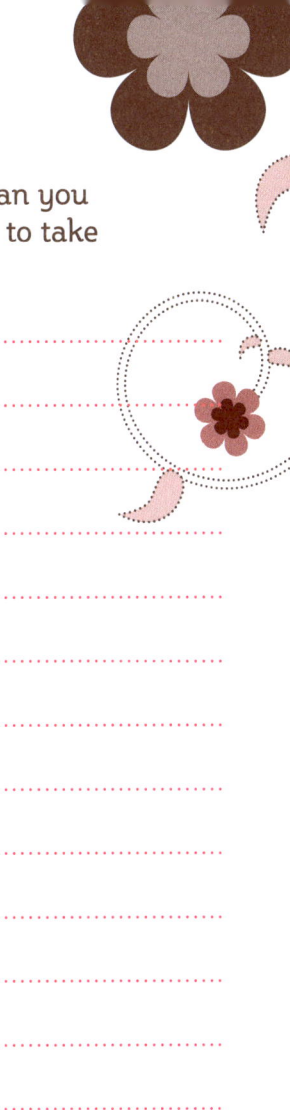

What can your partner do to support you right now? How can you support him? Think of things the two of you can do together to take your mind off the waiting.

# fertility treatment CYCLE 1

What kinds of things make you feel your best? Happiest? What special treats can you indulge in to help make the two weeks seem to go by faster? Make lists of things that will help you feel comforted and cared for while you're waiting, even if it's something as simple as meeting a friend for tea and sympathy.

If you feel yourself spiraling into fear or negativity, write down thoughts that will stop those feelings cold. Remind yourself that you're doing everything possible to get pregnant. And hang in there . . .

# fertility treatment CYCLE 2

# Week 1

| DATE | ○ cycle day ○ vitamin | MEDICATIONS |
|---|---|---|
| APPOINTMENTS / DOCTOR'S ORDERS | | Oral  Time  Name  Amount |
| | | Inj.  Time  Name  Amount |

| DATE | ○ cycle day ○ vitamin | MEDICATIONS |
|---|---|---|
| APPOINTMENTS / DOCTOR'S ORDERS | | Oral  Time  Name  Amount |
| | | Inj.  Time  Name  Amount |

| DATE | ○ cycle day ○ vitamin | MEDICATIONS |
|---|---|---|
| APPOINTMENTS / DOCTOR'S ORDERS | | Oral  Time  Name  Amount |
| | | Inj.  Time  Name  Amount |

## DATE .................... ( ) cycle day ( ) vitamin

### APPOINTMENTS / DOCTOR'S ORDERS

## MEDICATIONS

| Oral | Time | Name | Amount |
|---|---|---|---|
| ○ | | | |
| ○ | | | |

| Inj. | Time | Name | Amount |
|---|---|---|---|
| ○ | | | |
| ○ | | | |
| ○ | | | |
| ○ | | | |
| ○ | | | |

---

## DATE .................... ( ) cycle day ( ) vitamin

### APPOINTMENTS / DOCTOR'S ORDERS

## MEDICATIONS

| Oral | Time | Name | Amount |
|---|---|---|---|
| ○ | | | |
| ○ | | | |

| Inj. | Time | Name | Amount |
|---|---|---|---|
| ○ | | | |
| ○ | | | |
| ○ | | | |
| ○ | | | |
| ○ | | | |

---

## DATE .................... ( ) cycle day ( ) vitamin

### APPOINTMENTS / DOCTOR'S ORDERS

## MEDICATIONS

| Oral | Time | Name | Amount |
|---|---|---|---|
| ○ | | | |
| ○ | | | |

| Inj. | Time | Name | Amount |
|---|---|---|---|
| ○ | | | |
| ○ | | | |
| ○ | | | |
| ○ | | | |
| ○ | | | |

---

## DATE .................... ( ) cycle day ( ) vitamin

### APPOINTMENTS / DOCTOR'S ORDERS

## MEDICATIONS

| Oral | Time | Name | Amount |
|---|---|---|---|
| ○ | | | |
| ○ | | | |

| Inj. | Time | Name | Amount |
|---|---|---|---|
| ○ | | | |
| ○ | | | |
| ○ | | | |
| ○ | | | |
| ○ | | | |

## fertility treatment CYCLE 2

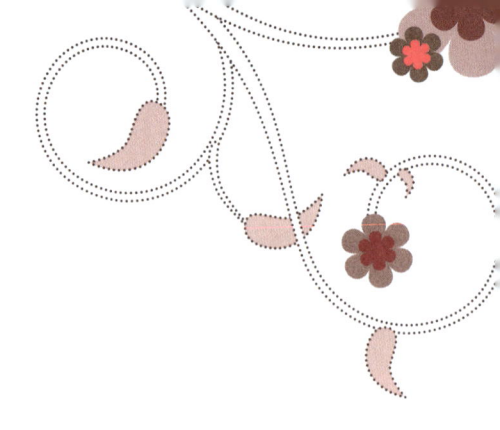

# Week 2

**DATE** .................... ◯ cycle day ◯ vitamin

APPOINTMENTS / DOCTOR'S ORDERS

**MEDICATIONS**

Oral   Time   Name   Amount

Inj.   Time   Name   Amount

---

**DATE** .................... ◯ cycle day ◯ vitamin

APPOINTMENTS / DOCTOR'S ORDERS

**MEDICATIONS**

Oral   Time   Name   Amount

Inj.   Time   Name   Amount

---

**DATE** .................... ◯ cycle day ◯ vitamin

APPOINTMENTS / DOCTOR'S ORDERS

**MEDICATIONS**

Oral   Time   Name   Amount

Inj.   Time   Name   Amount

## DATE .................... ◯ cycle day ◯ vitamin

### APPOINTMENTS / DOCTOR'S ORDERS

### MEDICATIONS

| Oral | Time | Name | Amount |
|---|---|---|---|
| ◯ | | | |
| ◯ | | | |

| Inj. | Time | Name | Amount |
|---|---|---|---|
| ◯ | | | |
| ◯ | | | |
| ◯ | | | |
| ◯ | | | |
| ◯ | | | |

---

## DATE .................... ◯ cycle day ◯ vitamin

### APPOINTMENTS / DOCTOR'S ORDERS

### MEDICATIONS

| Oral | Time | Name | Amount |
|---|---|---|---|
| ◯ | | | |
| ◯ | | | |

| Inj. | Time | Name | Amount |
|---|---|---|---|
| ◯ | | | |
| ◯ | | | |
| ◯ | | | |
| ◯ | | | |
| ◯ | | | |

---

## DATE .................... ◯ cycle day ◯ vitamin

### APPOINTMENTS / DOCTOR'S ORDERS

### MEDICATIONS

| Oral | Time | Name | Amount |
|---|---|---|---|
| ◯ | | | |
| ◯ | | | |

| Inj. | Time | Name | Amount |
|---|---|---|---|
| ◯ | | | |
| ◯ | | | |
| ◯ | | | |
| ◯ | | | |
| ◯ | | | |

---

## DATE .................... ◯ cycle day ◯ vitamin

### APPOINTMENTS / DOCTOR'S ORDERS

### MEDICATIONS

| Oral | Time | Name | Amount |
|---|---|---|---|
| ◯ | | | |
| ◯ | | | |

| Inj. | Time | Name | Amount |
|---|---|---|---|
| ◯ | | | |
| ◯ | | | |
| ◯ | | | |
| ◯ | | | |
| ◯ | | | |

# fertility treatment CYCLE 2

# Week 3

**DATE** .................... ( ) cycle day ( ) vitamin

**MEDICATIONS**

APPOINTMENTS / DOCTOR'S ORDERS

| Oral | Time | Name | Amount |
| Inj. | Time | Name | Amount |

**DATE** .................... ( ) cycle day ( ) vitamin

**MEDICATIONS**

APPOINTMENTS / DOCTOR'S ORDERS

| Oral | Time | Name | Amount |
| Inj. | Time | Name | Amount |

**DATE** .................... ( ) cycle day ( ) vitamin

**MEDICATIONS**

APPOINTMENTS / DOCTOR'S ORDERS

| Oral | Time | Name | Amount |
| Inj. | Time | Name | Amount |

## DATE ............ ⬚ cycle day ⬚ vitamin

**APPOINTMENTS / DOCTOR'S ORDERS**

### MEDICATIONS

| Oral | Time | Name | Amount |
|---|---|---|---|
| ⬚ | | | |
| ⬚ | | | |

| Inj. | Time | Name | Amount |
|---|---|---|---|
| ⬚ | | | |
| ⬚ | | | |
| ⬚ | | | |
| ⬚ | | | |
| ⬚ | | | |

---

## DATE ............ ⬚ cycle day ⬚ vitamin

**APPOINTMENTS / DOCTOR'S ORDERS**

### MEDICATIONS

| Oral | Time | Name | Amount |
|---|---|---|---|
| ⬚ | | | |
| ⬚ | | | |

| Inj. | Time | Name | Amount |
|---|---|---|---|
| ⬚ | | | |
| ⬚ | | | |
| ⬚ | | | |
| ⬚ | | | |
| ⬚ | | | |

---

## DATE ............ ⬚ cycle day ⬚ vitamin

**APPOINTMENTS / DOCTOR'S ORDERS**

### MEDICATIONS

| Oral | Time | Name | Amount |
|---|---|---|---|
| ⬚ | | | |
| ⬚ | | | |

| Inj. | Time | Name | Amount |
|---|---|---|---|
| ⬚ | | | |
| ⬚ | | | |
| ⬚ | | | |
| ⬚ | | | |
| ⬚ | | | |

---

## DATE ............ ⬚ cycle day ⬚ vitamin

**APPOINTMENTS / DOCTOR'S ORDERS**

### MEDICATIONS

| Oral | Time | Name | Amount |
|---|---|---|---|
| ⬚ | | | |
| ⬚ | | | |

| Inj. | Time | Name | Amount |
|---|---|---|---|
| ⬚ | | | |
| ⬚ | | | |
| ⬚ | | | |
| ⬚ | | | |
| ⬚ | | | |

**fertility treatment CYCLE 2**

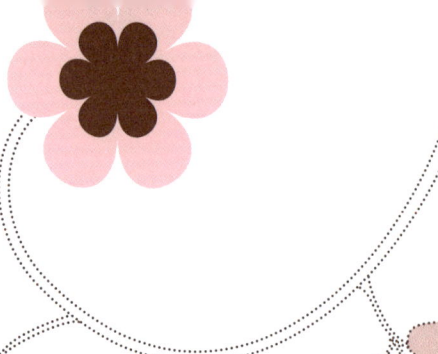

# Week 4

**DATE** _____ ( ) cycle day ( ) vitamin

APPOINTMENTS / DOCTOR'S ORDERS

**MEDICATIONS**

| Oral | Time | Name | Amount |
|---|---|---|---|

| Inj. | Time | Name | Amount |
|---|---|---|---|

---

**DATE** _____ ( ) cycle day ( ) vitamin

APPOINTMENTS / DOCTOR'S ORDERS

**MEDICATIONS**

| Oral | Time | Name | Amount |
|---|---|---|---|

| Inj. | Time | Name | Amount |
|---|---|---|---|

---

**DATE** _____ ( ) cycle day ( ) vitamin

APPOINTMENTS / DOCTOR'S ORDERS

**MEDICATIONS**

| Oral | Time | Name | Amount |
|---|---|---|---|

| Inj. | Time | Name | Amount |
|---|---|---|---|

# DATE ............... ◯ cycle day ◯ vitamin

## APPOINTMENTS / DOCTOR'S ORDERS

## MEDICATIONS

| Oral | Time | Name | Amount |
|---|---|---|---|
| ◯ | | | |
| ◯ | | | |

| Inj. | Time | Name | Amount |
|---|---|---|---|
| ◯ | | | |
| ◯ | | | |
| ◯ | | | |
| ◯ | | | |
| ◯ | | | |

---

# DATE ............... ◯ cycle day ◯ vitamin

## APPOINTMENTS / DOCTOR'S ORDERS

## MEDICATIONS

| Oral | Time | Name | Amount |
|---|---|---|---|
| ◯ | | | |
| ◯ | | | |

| Inj. | Time | Name | Amount |
|---|---|---|---|
| ◯ | | | |
| ◯ | | | |
| ◯ | | | |
| ◯ | | | |
| ◯ | | | |

---

# DATE ............... ◯ cycle day ◯ vitamin

## APPOINTMENTS / DOCTOR'S ORDERS

## MEDICATIONS

| Oral | Time | Name | Amount |
|---|---|---|---|
| ◯ | | | |
| ◯ | | | |

| Inj. | Time | Name | Amount |
|---|---|---|---|
| ◯ | | | |
| ◯ | | | |
| ◯ | | | |
| ◯ | | | |
| ◯ | | | |

---

# DATE ............... ◯ cycle day ◯ vitamin

## APPOINTMENTS / DOCTOR'S ORDERS

## MEDICATIONS

| Oral | Time | Name | Amount |
|---|---|---|---|
| ◯ | | | |
| ◯ | | | |

| Inj. | Time | Name | Amount |
|---|---|---|---|
| ◯ | | | |
| ◯ | | | |
| ◯ | | | |
| ◯ | | | |
| ◯ | | | |

**fertility treatment CYCLE 2**

# Week 5

**DATE** ............................. ( ) cycle day ( ) vitamin

**APPOINTMENTS / DOCTOR'S ORDERS**

**MEDICATIONS**

| Oral | Time | Name | Amount |
|---|---|---|---|
| ○ | | | |
| ○ | | | |

| Inj. | Time | Name | Amount |
|---|---|---|---|
| ○ | | | |
| ○ | | | |
| ○ | | | |
| ○ | | | |
| ○ | | | |

**DATE** ............................. ( ) cycle day ( ) vitamin

**APPOINTMENTS / DOCTOR'S ORDERS**

**MEDICATIONS**

| Oral | Time | Name | Amount |
|---|---|---|---|
| ○ | | | |
| ○ | | | |

| Inj. | Time | Name | Amount |
|---|---|---|---|
| ○ | | | |
| ○ | | | |
| ○ | | | |
| ○ | | | |
| ○ | | | |

**DATE** ............................. ( ) cycle day ( ) vitamin

**APPOINTMENTS / DOCTOR'S ORDERS**

**MEDICATIONS**

| Oral | Time | Name | Amount |
|---|---|---|---|
| ○ | | | |
| ○ | | | |

| Inj. | Time | Name | Amount |
|---|---|---|---|
| ○ | | | |
| ○ | | | |
| ○ | | | |
| ○ | | | |
| ○ | | | |

# DATE .................. ( ) cycle day ( ) vitamin

## APPOINTMENTS / DOCTOR'S ORDERS

## MEDICATIONS

| Oral | Time | Name | Amount |
|---|---|---|---|
| ○ | | | |
| ○ | | | |

| Inj. | Time | Name | Amount |
|---|---|---|---|
| ○ | | | |
| ○ | | | |
| ○ | | | |
| ○ | | | |
| ○ | | | |

---

# DATE .................. ( ) cycle day ( ) vitamin

## APPOINTMENTS / DOCTOR'S ORDERS

## MEDICATIONS

| Oral | Time | Name | Amount |
|---|---|---|---|
| ○ | | | |
| ○ | | | |

| Inj. | Time | Name | Amount |
|---|---|---|---|
| ○ | | | |
| ○ | | | |
| ○ | | | |
| ○ | | | |
| ○ | | | |

---

# DATE .................. ( ) cycle day ( ) vitamin

## APPOINTMENTS / DOCTOR'S ORDERS

## MEDICATIONS

| Oral | Time | Name | Amount |
|---|---|---|---|
| ○ | | | |
| ○ | | | |

| Inj. | Time | Name | Amount |
|---|---|---|---|
| ○ | | | |
| ○ | | | |
| ○ | | | |
| ○ | | | |
| ○ | | | |

---

# DATE .................. ( ) cycle day ( ) vitamin

## APPOINTMENTS / DOCTOR'S ORDERS

## MEDICATIONS

| Oral | Time | Name | Amount |
|---|---|---|---|
| ○ | | | |
| ○ | | | |

| Inj. | Time | Name | Amount |
|---|---|---|---|
| ○ | | | |
| ○ | | | |
| ○ | | | |
| ○ | | | |
| ○ | | | |

# fertility treatment CYCLE 2

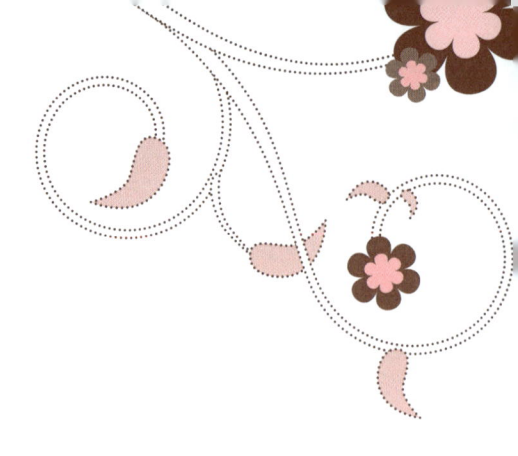

# Week 6

| DATE | cycle day | vitamin | MEDICATIONS |
|---|---|---|---|
APPOINTMENTS / DOCTOR'S ORDERS

Oral  Time  Name  Amount

Inj.  Time  Name  Amount

---

DATE ____ cycle day ____ vitamin

APPOINTMENTS / DOCTOR'S ORDERS

MEDICATIONS

Oral  Time  Name  Amount

Inj.  Time  Name  Amount

---

DATE ____ cycle day ____ vitamin

APPOINTMENTS / DOCTOR'S ORDERS

MEDICATIONS

Oral  Time  Name  Amount

Inj.  Time  Name  Amount

# DATE ............... ( ) cycle day ( ) vitamin

**APPOINTMENTS / DOCTOR'S ORDERS**

## MEDICATIONS

| Oral | Time | Name | Amount |
|---|---|---|---|
| ( ) | | | |
| ( ) | | | |

| Inj. | Time | Name | Amount |
|---|---|---|---|
| ( ) | | | |
| ( ) | | | |
| ( ) | | | |
| ( ) | | | |
| ( ) | | | |

---

# DATE ............... ( ) cycle day ( ) vitamin

**APPOINTMENTS / DOCTOR'S ORDERS**

## MEDICATIONS

| Oral | Time | Name | Amount |
|---|---|---|---|
| ( ) | | | |
| ( ) | | | |

| Inj. | Time | Name | Amount |
|---|---|---|---|
| ( ) | | | |
| ( ) | | | |
| ( ) | | | |
| ( ) | | | |
| ( ) | | | |

---

# DATE ............... ( ) cycle day ( ) vitamin

**APPOINTMENTS / DOCTOR'S ORDERS**

## MEDICATIONS

| Oral | Time | Name | Amount |
|---|---|---|---|
| ( ) | | | |
| ( ) | | | |

| Inj. | Time | Name | Amount |
|---|---|---|---|
| ( ) | | | |
| ( ) | | | |
| ( ) | | | |
| ( ) | | | |
| ( ) | | | |

---

# DATE ............... ( ) cycle day ( ) vitamin

**APPOINTMENTS / DOCTOR'S ORDERS**

## MEDICATIONS

| Oral | Time | Name | Amount |
|---|---|---|---|
| ( ) | | | |
| ( ) | | | |

| Inj. | Time | Name | Amount |
|---|---|---|---|
| ( ) | | | |
| ( ) | | | |
| ( ) | | | |
| ( ) | | | |
| ( ) | | | |

fertility treatment CYCLE 2

## It's Very Frustrating (IVF)

*Why me? Why haven't I been able to get pregnant?* You probably started thinking this a long time ago, but now that you're on your second IVF cycle, it's a recurring theme. Many women blame themselves, and think they must have done something wrong. They feel guilty and ashamed that they can't do something they believe should be natural and effortless. Some say they feel like less of a woman, or they worry that their partner will love them less if they can't produce a child.

If you're feeling any of those things . . . stop those thoughts immediately! Fertility problems have many causes, and most are unrelated to anything you did or didn't do. And, of course, fertility problems are as common in men as in women, so your progression to IVF may have more to do with your partner than yourself. In either case, there's no use assigning blame, self or otherwise.

Rewrite the negative script in your head. You are more than your fertility. Instead of thinking you're somehow less of a woman because you're having trouble getting pregnant, use these pages to remind yourself of all the ways you're a wonderful woman—as well as a wonder wife, daughter, friend, and sister. And know that someday you'll be a wonderful mother, too.

In time, you will be a mother. What have you learned from the journey to conception that will help make you a better parent?

................................................................................

What achievements in your life are you most proud of?

................................................................................

# fertility treatment CYCLE 2

What makes you a terrific person?

List all your best qualities and all the reasons you know you'll be a great mother:

List all the reasons why he'll be a terrific father:

..........................................................................................
..........................................................................................
..........................................................................................
..........................................................................................
..........................................................................................
..........................................................................................
..........................................................................................
..........................................................................................
..........................................................................................

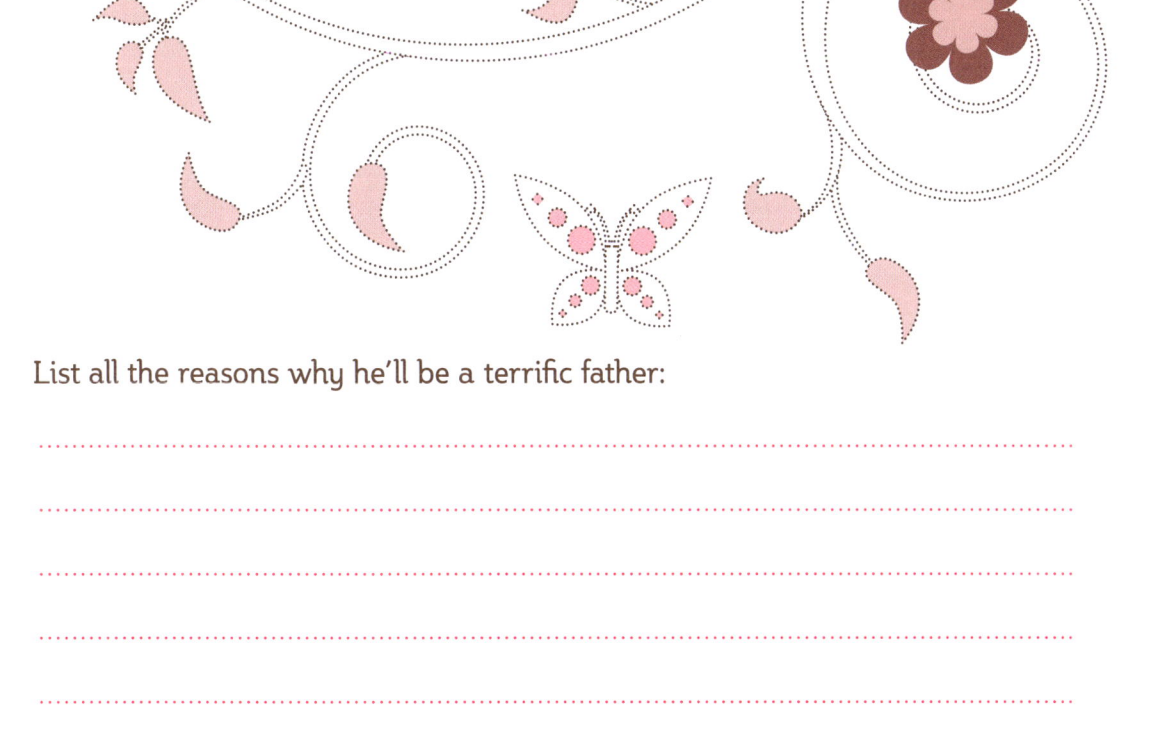

# What Comes Next

Your hopes are still high, and they should be. You could be pregnant right now!

But it's also smart to protect yourself by considering what's next if this cycle isn't successful. You'll want to talk to your partner about when it's time to switch gears. Fertility treatments can take an emotional toll, and one way to avoid burn-out is to have a strategy for how to move on.

Start by thinking about what's more important to you: becoming pregnant, or becoming a parent. Because you can be a parent, whether or not this IVF cycle is successful. You might decide you want to try IVF again, or you might want to explore a whole world—literally—of possibilities for becoming a parent. Third-party reproduction (egg donors, sperm donors, surrogates, and gestational carriers) and adoption are all beautiful ways to form a family. Or perhaps you'll consider remaining child-free. Only you and your partner can decide what kind of family you want to create. The important thing is recognizing that you can create it.

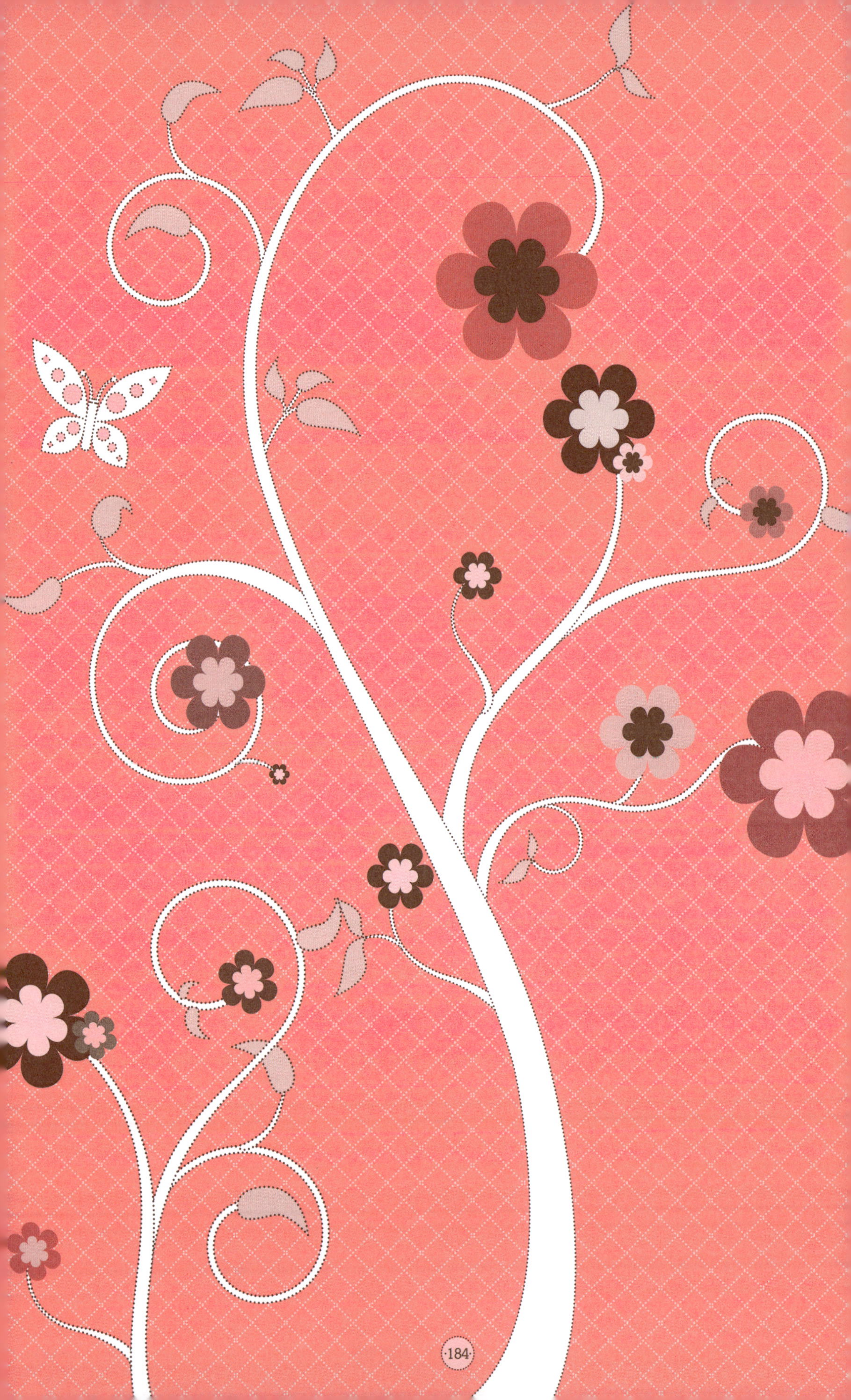

# Baby on the Way

## Congratulations!
All your conception planning has paid off, and you're pregnant! The next nine months are going to be amazing. Now that you're expecting, you've got a whole new kind of planning to do so that your pregnancy—and your baby—are as healthy as possible.

One of the first things most new expectant moms want to know is what they need to change about their lifestyle right away. The more planning and preparation you did before you got pregnant, the less you'll have to change now. It's never too late to take steps for a healthy pregnancy. So if you haven't already done so . . .

○ Stop smoking and drinking alcohol immediately. Both can jeopardize your baby's health. And it goes without saying that illegal/recreational drugs are a big no-no.

○ Check your medications. Even before your first prenatal appointment you'll want to know that any medications you're taking are safe during pregnancy.

○ Start taking prenatal vitamins, or one-a-day-type vitamins containing folic acid.

○ Try to avoid exposure to chemicals such as paints, paint thinners, pesticides, solvents, formaldehyde, etc. If your job exposes you to hazardous substances, talk to your doctor and then see if you can at least temporarily switch assignments so you're not around these chemicals.

# baby on the way

Next, call and make an appointment for your first prenatal checkup. If you're in good health and you conceived fairly quickly, your appointment may not be for several weeks. But women who have an existing health condition, or who had problems conceiving, may want to see a doctor sooner.

If you've been seeing a gynecologist you like, and he or she is also a practicing obstetrician, you're way ahead of the game. But many gynecologists no longer deliver babies, so you might need to look for a new doctor now that you're pregnant.

Your current doctor will no doubt have recommendations of good obstetricians in your area, and you should also ask friends and family members whose opinions you trust. Once you have some names, here are a few things to check:

○ Make sure the doctor is board certified in obstetrics. You can call the American College of Obstetrics and Gynecology at 202-638-5577 or visit www.ACOG.org/member-lookup to check.

○ Make sure your health insurance plan covers the doctor you want to see.

○ If the doctor is part of a group practice, ask if you will be seeing all the doctors, and whether or not you can choose who will be present at your delivery. If not, try to meet all the doctors in the practice before you sign on.

○ Find out which hospital the doctor is affiliated with. You'll be making many visits to the doctor's office for checkups, but you'll be making one very important visit to the hospital for your delivery. Make sure the hospital's location is convenient and that the facilities are up-to-date. If your pregnancy is high-risk for any reason (health problem, age, etc.), check that the hospital has a well-equipped NICU (neonatal intensive care unit) in case there are any problems.

You're probably not going to see much change in your belly until around the eight week mark or so. Your breasts may start swelling by then, too. But even then it might just seem as if you're a bit bloated, like a bad case of PMS.

If you generally wear very tailored or form-fitting fashions, you may find that your clothes are getting snug before the end of the first trimester (three months). If you tend to wear more loose or flowing clothing, you may make it well into the second trimester before you have to go out and get new clothes.

As happy as you are to be pregnant, you probably won't love the first pregnancy symptoms you experience: fatigue and nausea. So-called morning sickness can actually occur at any time of the day or night, and can range from mild queasiness to vomiting so severe that it requires hospitalization (this is very rare). In fact, an estimated 80 percent of pregnant women experience pregnancy nausea, which is considered a perfectly normal part of pregnancy.

If you've got that queasy feeling, here are some things that may help:

○ Make sure you get lots of sleep (obviously that will help with pregnancy fatigue, too).

○ Try switching from three big meals a day to five or six smaller ones.

○ If you're having trouble keeping food down, don't worry too much about what you're supposed to eat, and just go with whatever appeals. For instance, if broccoli makes you sick but blueberry muffins don't upset your stomach, eat the blueberry muffins. There will be time after the nausea subsides for you to get your pregnancy nutrition on track.

○ Drink plenty of fluids to keep yourself hydrated, especially if you're vomiting. But try not to drink for at least 30 minutes after eating, as that can aggravate the nausea.

○ Avoid unpleasant odors.

○ Don't wear clothing that puts any pressure on your waist or abdomen.

Happily, both nausea and fatigue usually fade after the third month. If not, ask your doctor about pregnancy-safe medications that might help.

Other early pregnancy symptoms you may experience, all perfectly normal, include tender breasts, frequent urination, and hot flashes.

Obviously there's lots and lots of information available on pregnancy symptoms, weight gain, lifestyle changes, delivery options, medical tests, and more. What was listed here are just the highlights of what you can expect early in your pregnancy, and what you need to do right away to give your baby a healthy start. But you've got lots more reading to do, and lots more planning, too. So go out and buy a pregnancy journal now so you can continue to keep track of this amazing journey. We wish you a very happy and healthy pregnancy!

# questions for your doctor

As you read and fill out this journal, you may have questions pertaining to your own situation that you want to ask your doctor. Write them down here so you don't forget, and then bring the journal with you to your next medical appointment. That way you can jot the answers down as soon as you get them.

Q

A

Q

A

Q

A

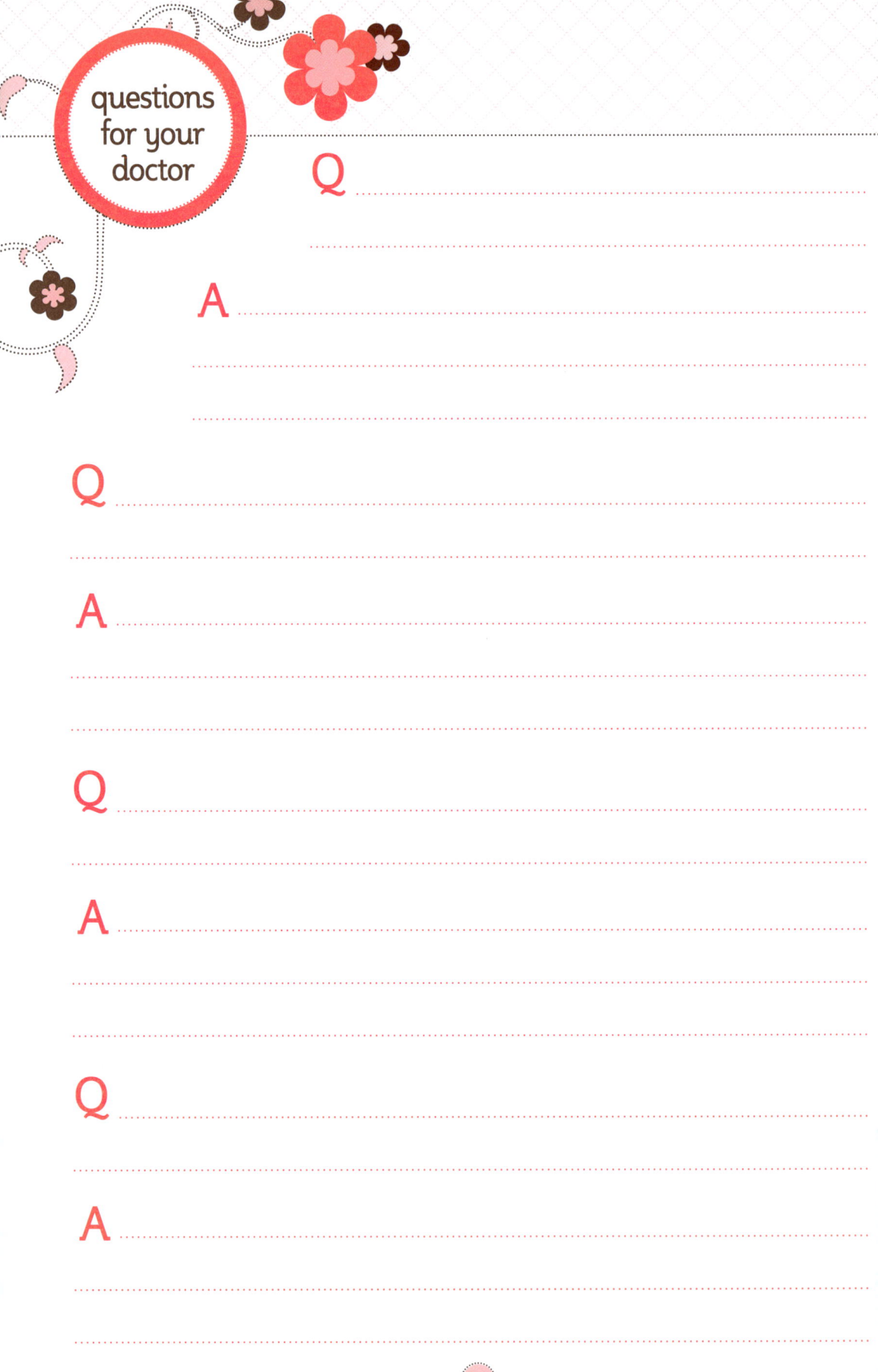

## questions for your doctor

Q

A

Q

A

Q

A

Q

A

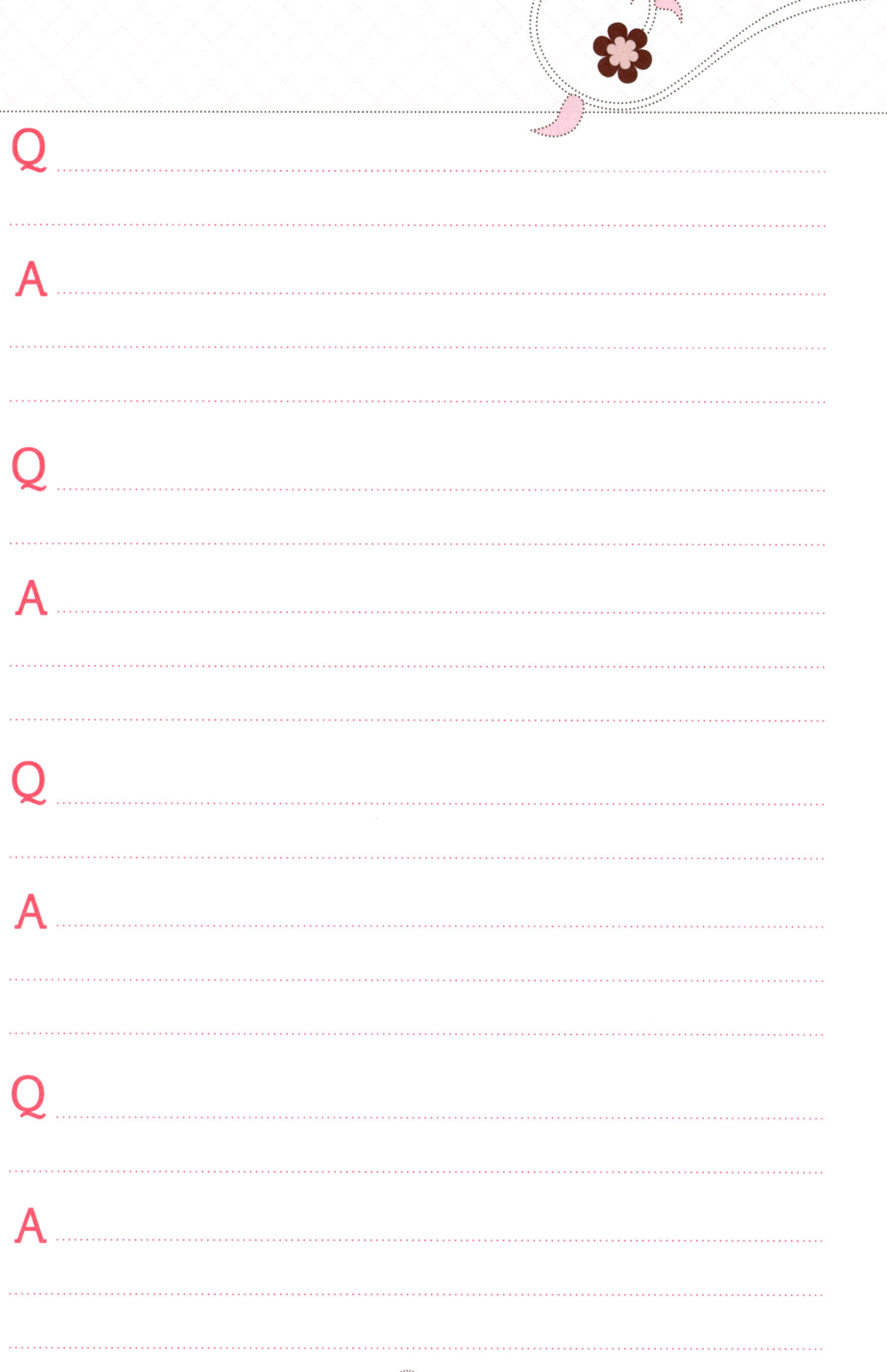

Q

A

Q

A

Q

A

Q

A

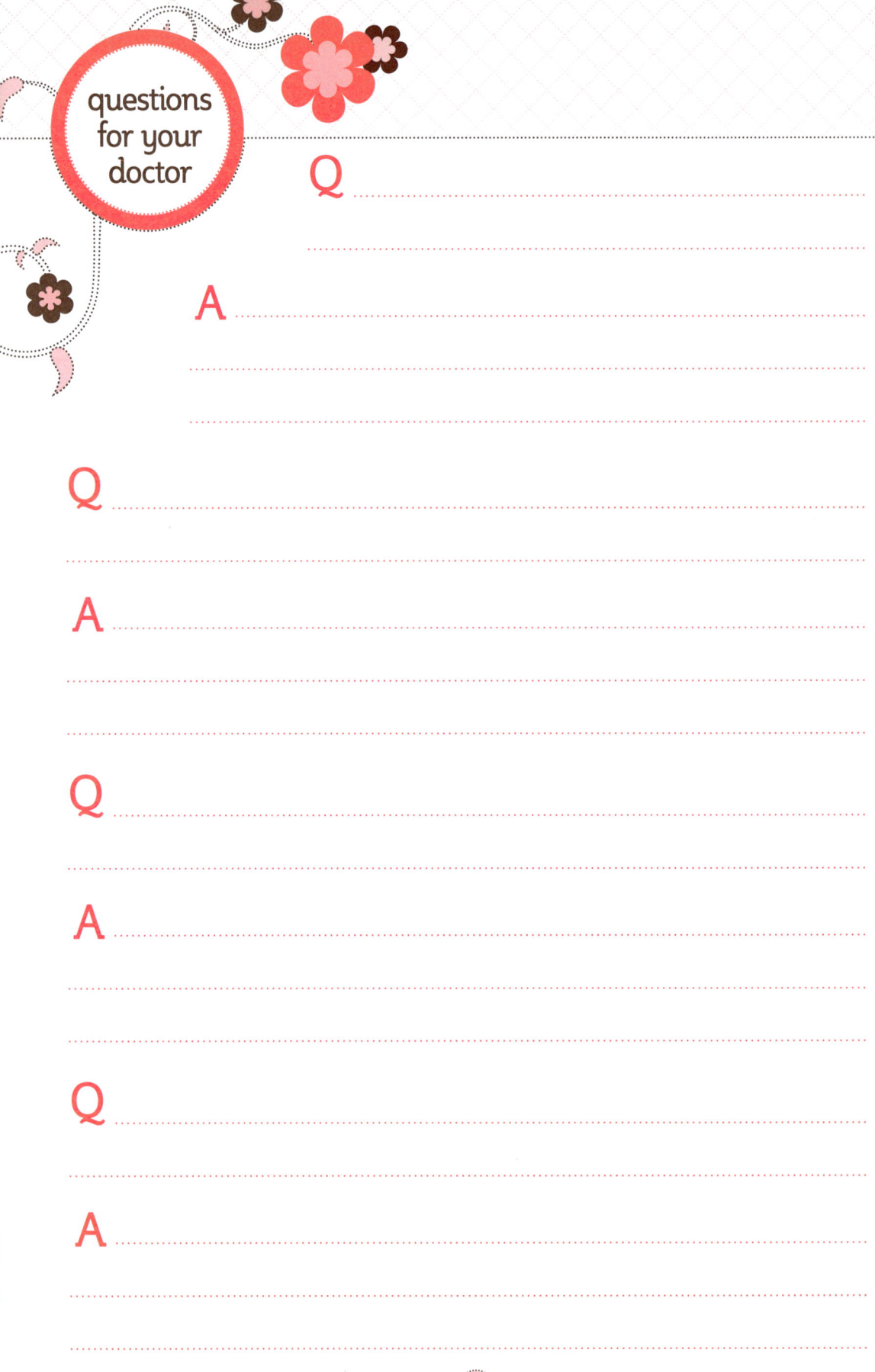

## questions for your doctor

Q

A

Q

A

Q

A

Q

A

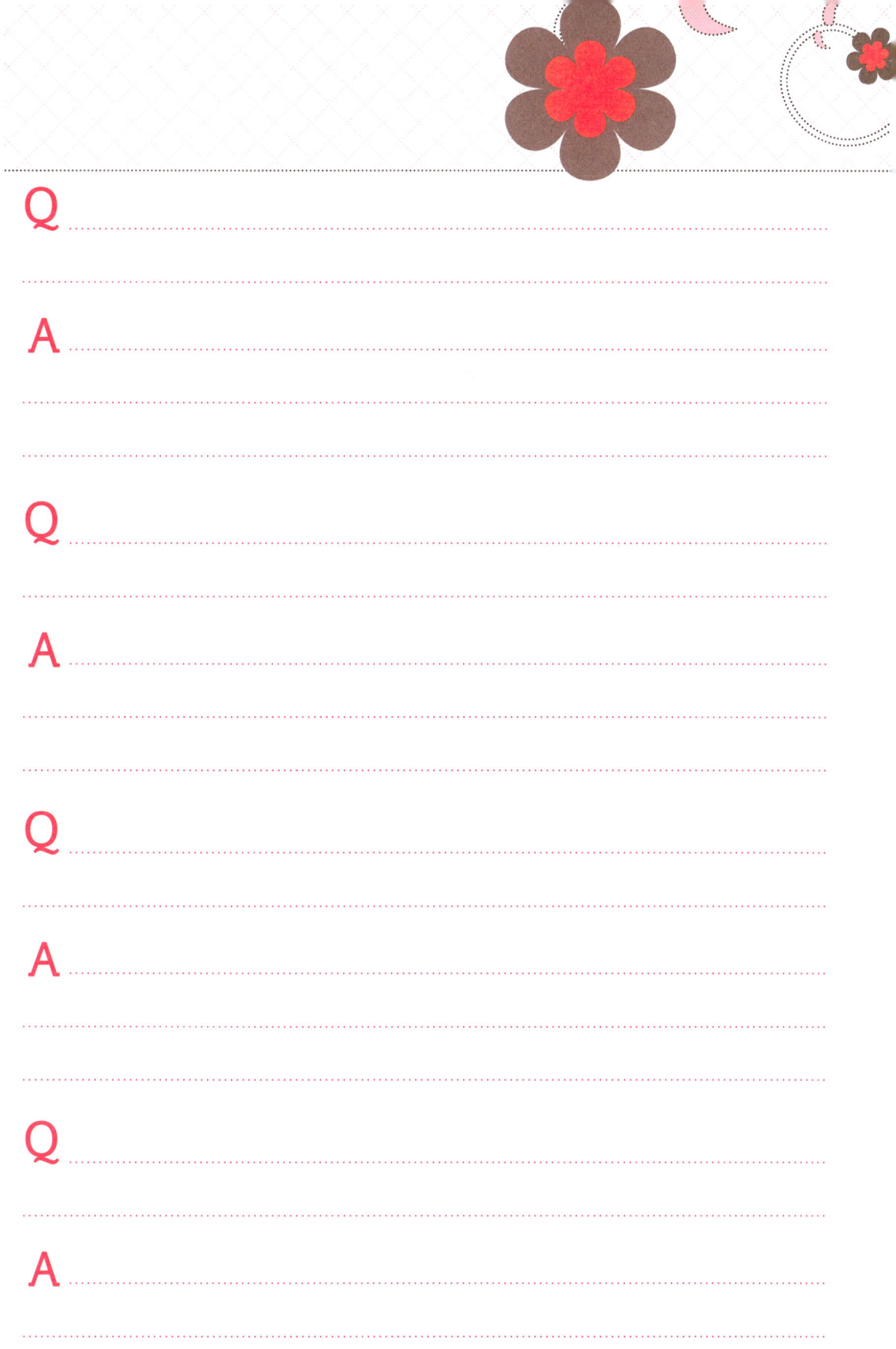

Q

A


Q


A


Q


A


Q


A

# contacts

Use these pages to jot down the names of your various specialists: doctors, nurses, pharmacists, counselors or therapists, yoga instructors, acupuncturists, and herbalists, and anyone else who is helping you on your journey.

NAME

ADDRESS

PHONE          WORK          CELL

E-MAIL

NAME

ADDRESS

PHONE          WORK          CELL

E-MAIL

NAME

ADDRESS

PHONE          WORK          CELL

E-MAIL

NAME

ADDRESS

PHONE          WORK          CELL

E-MAIL

# contacts

NAME

ADDRESS


PHONE         WORK                CELL

E-MAIL


NAME

ADDRESS


PHONE         WORK                CELL

E-MAIL


NAME

ADDRESS


PHONE         WORK                CELL

E-MAIL


NAME

ADDRESS


PHONE         WORK                CELL

E-MAIL

NAME

ADDRESS

PHONE                    WORK                         CELL

E-MAIL

NAME

ADDRESS

PHONE                    WORK                         CELL

E-MAIL

NAME

ADDRESS

PHONE                    WORK                         CELL

E-MAIL

NAME

ADDRESS

PHONE                    WORK                         CELL

E-MAIL

# resources

This fertility journal provides information about natural conception and various kinds of fertility treatments, including ART (assisted reproductive technology, which includes in vitro fertilization). For anyone who wants more information than can fit in these pages, there are other resources available.

To start with, check out *Conceive*'s special fertility journal Web site, www.conceivefertilityjournal.com, that provides more in-depth content on some of the topics covered in this book. On this site you can find a BMI (body mass index) calculator, lists of safe seafood and foods with a low glycemic index, additional information on ovulation monitors and fitness programs for fertility, and lots more.

There are also other Web sites, organizations, and books that can provide more specific information if you need it. Here are a few to check out (keep in mind that none of these, of course, is a substitute for medical advice):

## ORGANIZATIONS AND WEB SITES

**Conceive Magazine** www.conceiveonline.com
*Conceive Magazine* and *Conceive Online* provide information and support for women at any stage of family-building.

**American Academy of Obstetricians and Gynecologists (ACOG)** www.acog.org
The Web site of this national organization of women's health care physicians provides patient information on all aspects of reproduction.

**The American Fertility Association (AFA)** www.theafa.org
The AFA, a not-for-profit organization, provides information about infertility treatments, reproductive and sexual health, and family-building options.

**American Society for Reproductive Medicine (ASRM)** www.asrm.org
An organization of specialists in reproductive medicine, the ASRM's Web site provides a wealth of information on infertility and its treatments.

**Centers for Disease Control and Prevention (CDC)** www.cdc.gov/ncbddd/preconception
This is a government agency site for a preconception care public health campaign urging women of reproductive age to get themselves healthy before becoming pregnant. A good resource for general and reproductive health information.

**Fertile Hope** www.fertilehope.org
This nonprofit organization is dedicated to helping cancer patients faced with infertility.

**Fertility LifeLines** www.fertilitylifelines.com, 1-866-LETS-TRY
An educational service provided by Serono, a pharmaceutical company. Callers to Fertility LifeLines speak to representatives, including nurse specialists, who can answer questions about fertility health concerns.

**The InterNational Council on Infertility Information Dissemination (INCIID)** www.inciid.org
INCIID (pronounced "inside") is a nonprofit organization that helps individuals and couples explore their family-building options. INCIID also offers scholarships for families needing financial support to consider IVF.

# resources

**March of Dimes** www.marchofdimes.com
This not-for-profit organization improves the health of babies by encouraging preconception health and preventing birth defects, premature birth, and infant mortality through research, community services, and advocacy.

**RESOLVE: The National Infertility Association** www.resolve.org
Resolve is a nonprofit organization for men and women experiencing infertility or other reproductive disorders. The group has a network of chapters nationwide to promote reproductive health and raise awareness of infertility issues and family-building options.

# BOOKS
## General reproductive health and natural conception:

*The Everything Getting Pregnant Book*
By Robin Elise Weiss (Adams Media Corporation, 2004)
Weiss, a certified childbirth educator, outlines the path to pregnancy, from going off birth control to considering fertility treatments when conception doesn't happen naturally.

*Fertility and Conception*
By Zita West (DK Adult, 2003)
A well-known British midwife (also author of *Plan to Get Pregnant,* DK Adult, 2008) with a holistic approach, West provides advice for couples who are newly trying as well as those who are experiencing problems. The book also discusses fertility treatment options, including IVF, neatly bridging the divide between conventional medicine and alternative treatments.

*Fertility Facts*
By Kim Hahn and the Editors of *Conceive Magazine* (Chronicle Books, 2008)
A compendium of 250 facts about reproduction, providing instant knowledge about diet, exercise, lifestyle, fertility treatments, and other factors that can influence conception.

*The Mother of All Pregnancy Books*
By Ann Douglas (Wiley, 2002)
A remarkably well-researched and comprehensive book that begins with information for couples considering pregnancy and continues through to breast-feeding.

*Preconception Plain and Simple*
By Audrey Couto McClelland and Sharon K. Couto (Pinks and Blues Publishing, 2005)
A fun book for couples just embarking on the fertility journey, this mother-daughter team of authors provides information on promoting fertility with foods, flowers, aromas, gemstones, and amulets. The idea is to follow the usual medical advice (provided in the book), and then add a bit of romance and relaxation to conception.

*Taking Charge of Your Fertility*
By Toni Weschler, M.P.H. (Collins, Tenth Anniversary Edition, 2006)
This classic fertility tome explains how to use the fertility awareness method (FAM) to achieve pregnancy, or avoid it. By observing various fertility signs such as morning temperature and cervical mucus, women learn to determine when they are ovulating.

# Fertility challenges:
## Conquering Infertility
By Alice D. Domar, Ph.D., and Alice Lesch Kelly (Penguin, 2004)
Domar, an assistant professor of medicine at Harvard, gives women the tools they need to deal with the stress that can undermine fertility or arise from infertility. Topics include relaxation techniques such as yoga, meditation, journal writing, and guided imagery.

## The Fertile Female
By Julia Indichova (Adell Press, 2007)
Indichova, also author of *Inconceivable: A Woman's Triumph over Despair and Statistics* (Broadway, 2001), espouses a hopeful and empowering view of female fertility. The book includes nurturing advice as well as information on a fertility-friendly lifestyle and diet (including recipes).

## I Am More Than My Infertility
By Marina Lombardo and Linda J. Parker (Seeds of Growth Press, 2007)
Lombardo, *Conceive Magazine's* "Emotionally Speaking" columnist, provides information and psychological support for women dealing with fertility challenges.

## The Infertility Answer Book
By Brette McWhorter Sember (Sphinx Publishing, 2005)
Sember, an attorney, has written a comprehensive book with answers to many of the legal questions surrounding fertility treatments, third-party reproduction (donor egg, donor sperm, surrogates, and gestational carriers), and adoption. Along with medical advice, this book can help couples decide how to proceed when natural conception doesn't work.

## The Infertility Cure
By Randine Lewis (Little, Brown and Company, 2005)
Lewis is a licensed acupuncturist and herbalist, and her book espouses Chinese medicine as an alternative to conventional Western treatments.

# Fertility treatments, including IVF:
## Conceptions and Misconceptions
By Arthur L. Wisot, M.D., and David R. Meldrum, M.D. (Hartley and Marks Publishers, revised and expanded second edition, 2004)
Two fertility specialists guide readers through the world of high-tech reproductive treatments, including tips for evaluating infertility clinics.

## In Vitro Fertilization: The A.R.T. of Making Babies
By Geoffrey Sher, M.D., Virginia Marriage Davis, R.N., M.N., and Jean Stoess, M.A. (Facts on File, third edition, 2005)
A complete guide to IVF, including information for couples on how to determine whether they're eligible, how to select a program, and an in-depth guide to how it works.

## What to Do When You Can't Get Pregnant
By Daniel A. Potter, M.D., and Jennifer S. Hanin, M.D. (Marlow & Company, 2005)
This book outlines all the reasons why couples may have trouble conceiving naturally, and then all the low- and high-tech methods available to help. There's also a fascinating chapter on future and experimental technologies, such as cloning.

# index

# A–C

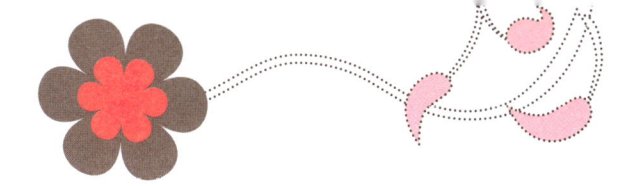

acronyms, used in fertility clinics, 149
alcohol consumption, 10-11, 56-57
bad habits, breaking, 52-53
basal body temperature (BBT), 16-17
    charting, 16-17
biological clock, 143
birth control. *See* contraception
birth control pills, 19-20
    polycystic ovary syndrome (PCOS) and, 19, 45
BMI (body mass index), 13-14, 16
    calculating, 14, 65
books, recommended, 200-201
caffeine, limiting intake of, 10-11, 58-59
calcium, requirements during pregnancy, 45
carbohydrates, 40, 41
cervical mucus and ovulation, 18
chasteberry (vitex), 14, 15
coffee drinking, 10-11, 27, 58-59
conception. *See also* miscarriage
    average time it takes, 10
    body weight and, 66
    books recommended, 200-201
    contraception and, 19-20
    eat to conceive, 12-13, 32-33
contacts, worksheets to use, 195-197
contraception, 20
    birth control pills and, 19-20
    conception and, 19-20
    Depo-Provera, 20
    hormonal contraception and, 20

# D–F

dental health, importance of, 29
diabetes, 10, 21
diet and nutrition. *See also* foods
    eat to conceive, 12-13, 32-33
    fatty acids, 12-13
    healthy diet, 11, 35, 36
    men eating healthy, 84-85
drugs, illegal, 60-61
endometriosis, 10, 19, 145
exercise
    benefits of regular, 102, 105
    fertility and, 106, 108, 110
    journal questions, 103, 105
    men and, 86-87
    tips for, 102-111
fatty acids, 12-13
fertility. *See also* male infertility
    age it begins declining, 143-144
    books recommended, 199-201
    boosting, 12-16
    common roadblocks to, 144-148
    consulting a doctor, 144
    exercise, positive benefits of, 106, 108
    fertility workup, 147-148
    overweight, impact on, 13-14
    smoking and, 11, 12, 54
    stress, effect of, 94, 97, 98
    underweight, impact on, 13-14, 69
fertility monitor, using, 18
folic acid, 11-12, 42, 46
foods. *See also* diet and nutrition
    fruits and vegetables, 12
    glycemic index, foods with a low, 12
    whole grains, 12
friendships, importance of girlfriends, 120
    bonding with other moms-to-be, 120
    journal questions, 121

# G–I

glycemic index, foods with a low, 12
gynecologist, consulting with, 144
Hahn, Kim (author), about, 206
herbal products, 60
humor, maintaining a sense of, 128-129

# index

journal questions, 129
in vitro fertilization (IVF), 145, 149, 197
    books recommended, 197
    Cycle 1 (6 weeks) calendar pages, 152-163
    Cycle 2 (6 weeks) calendar pages, 168-179, 180, 181
    embryos implanted (two week wait), 164-167
    how it works, 148, 151
    journal questions, 165-167
    tracking medications, 151
infertility. *See also* fertility; male infertility
    common reasons for, 144-148
    obstructions, 145
    polycystic ovary disease and, 145
    varicoceles, 145-146
intrauterine insemination (IUI), 148, 149
IVF. *See* in vitro fertilization

## L–N

lifestyle issues, 10-11
male infertility, 10, 91, 144. *See also* fertility
    cell phones and, 88
    common reasons for, 145-147
    diet considerations, 84-85
    heat, impact on testicles and, 86, 88-89, 146-147
    regular exercise, impact on, 86-87
    testing for, 147
    varicoceles, 145-146
medical history, 10, 24
    family medical history, 10, 26
medical tests, 30, 31
    blood tests, 30
    genetic tests, 30, 31
    ultrasound, 30
medications, 31
    organizing and tracking, 151
menstrual cycle, 15-16
    irregular, 144
miscarriage, 19, 20-21, 47
    causes why occur, 21
morning sickness, 41, 50, 129
motherhood, tips for impending, 136, 140-141
    working moms, 140-141
nutritional supplements, 14, 42-43, 51

## O–R

OB/GYN doctor, 10
    prenatal appointment (worksheet), 22-23
    worksheet to use to write down questions, 188-193
organizations, list of, 199-200
overweight, being
    fertility and, 13-14
ovulation, 16-18
    basal body temperature and, 16-17
    how triggered, 97
    irregular, 144
    menstrual cycle and, 15-16
    methods to calculate, 16-18
pampering yourself, tips for, 112-118
    getting over guilt about, 114
    inexpensive indulgences, 118
    journal questions, 113, 115, 117
parenthood, tips for impending, 132-141
    challenge of, 134-135
    journal questions, 133, 135, 137, 181-183
partner, relationship with
    communication, importance of, 124-125
    journal questions, 123, 126-127, 129
    romance, 76, 126-127
    tips for, 122-131
pets, 138, 139
polycystic ovary syndrome (PCOS), 10, 21, 110
    birth control pills and, 19, 145
pregnancy. *See also* conception; miscarriage
    cautions, 95, 119, 139

exercise during, 104, 106, 109-111
healthy eating, 34, 37, 38
men and, 89, 125, 130
morning sickness, 41, 50, 129
pampering yourself, 115, 116
physical changes, 186-187
prenatal exam, 22-24, 186
sex and, 75, 77, 79, 127
sleep, importance of, 99
steps to take for a healthy, 185-187
support, finding with other moms-to-be, 120
vitamins and nutritional needs, 11, 44-50
weight gain during, 64, 67, 69, 70
prenatal appointment, 22-24, 186
reproductive endocrinologist, 146-148
reproductive system, 11, 199-200
male and female (illustrated), 11
resources, 198-201
books, 200-201
organizations and Web sites, 199-200

## S–T

sexual intercourse, 72-73, 77, 80
fertile days, having sex during, 15-16, 17, 74, 75
journal questions, 73
keeping it romantic, 76, 126-127
sexually transmitted diseases (STDs), 24-25
scarring from infections, 10, 91, 145
smoking, 11, 12, 54-55, 90-91
sperm count, 16
factors that impact, 146
foods that might improve, 85
intracytoplasmic sperm injection (ICSI), 147, 149
testing, 147
spina bifida, 11, 12
stress, tips for reducing, 14-15, 92-101
journal questions, 93, 100

thyroid problems, getting under control, 10
trans fats, 13, 39

## U–V–W

uterine fibroids, 145
vacation, benefits of taking a, 80, 81
vaccinations, 28, 29
varicoceles, 145-146
vitamins, 11-12, 42-43, 46
nutritional supplements, 14, 42-43, 51
prenatal, 11, 48-49
Web sites, recommended, 199-200
weight, 13-14
BMI and, 13-14
diets and, 70, 71
fertility and, 13-14, 69
worksheets, 62-63
worksheets (12 months), 22-141

# About Kim Hahn

Kim Hahn is the founder and CEO of *Conceive Magazine* and the online radio show, Conceive On-Air. A former banking executive, Kim became disillusioned by the lack of consumer-friendly information available when she and her husband were trying to start their family. After Kim and her husband adopted a baby girl, Kim decided that she'd help provide information to other women facing the same issues.

Kim left her executive position to start *Conceive Magazine*, the first mainstream magazine for women who are hoping to start or expand their families. *Conceive*'s readers may be trying to conceive naturally, struggling to negotiate the maze of fertility tests and treatments, or planning to adopt. Kim's own experiences also helped her recognize the need for a fertility journal that was full of valuable information, and also contained space for women to personalize the pages to organize and chronicle their own journey to parenthood.

Kim received her MBA from the Crummer Graduate School of Business at Rollins College in Orlando, Florida. She serves on advisory boards for the International Council for Infertility Information Dissemination (INCIID), the Centers for Disease Control and Prevention, the March of Dimes, and the University of Florida. Her vision for *Conceive* and its sister companies is that they will use all forms of media to meet the needs of future parents.